Quest for the Sacred Stone

Quest for the Sacred Stone

An African tale of mystery and adventure

CICELY VAN STRATEN

OXFORD
UNIVERSITY PRESS

OXFORD
UNIVERSITY PRESS

Great Clarendon Street, Oxford OX2 6DP, United Kingdom

Oxford University Press is a department of the University of Oxford.
It furthers the University's objective of excellence in research, scholarship,
and education by publishing worldwide in

Oxford   New York

Athens   Auckland   Bangkok   Bogotá   Buenos Aires   Calcutta
Cape Town   Chennai   Dar es Salaam   Delhi   Florence   Hong Kong
Istanbul   Karachi   Kuala Lumpur   Madrid   Melbourne   Mexico City
Mumbai   Nairobi   Paris   São Paulo   Shanghai   Singapore   Taipei
Tokyo   Toronto   Warsaw

and associated companies in   Berlin   Ibadan

Oxford is a registered trademark of Oxford University Press
in the UK and certain other countries

Quest for the Sacred Stone
ISBN 0 19 571779 1

Commissioning editor: Daphne Paizee
Editor: Hettie Scholtz, Sharon Hughes
Cover designers: Chris Davis and Anne-Marie Berry
Illustrators: Anne Westoby (maps), Peter van Straten (frontispiece),
Chip Snaddon (cover)

Published by Oxford University Press Southern Africa
PO Box 12119, N1 City, 7463, Cape Town, South Africa

Set in 11 pt on 13.5 pt Minion by RHT desktop publishing cc, Durbanville
Reproduction by RHT desktop publishing cc, Durbanville
Cover reproduction by The Image Bureau
Printed and bound by Creda Communications

The plains where Tajewo and Meramo live

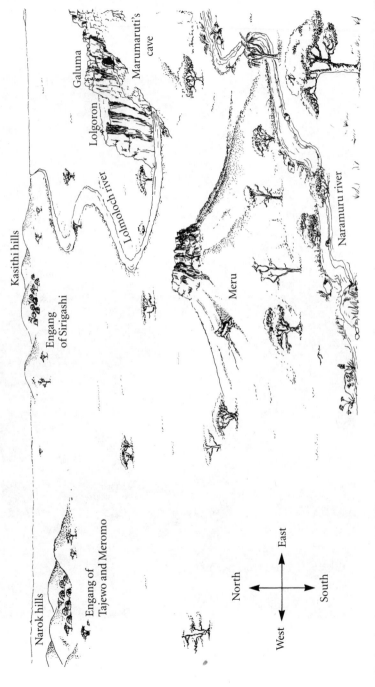

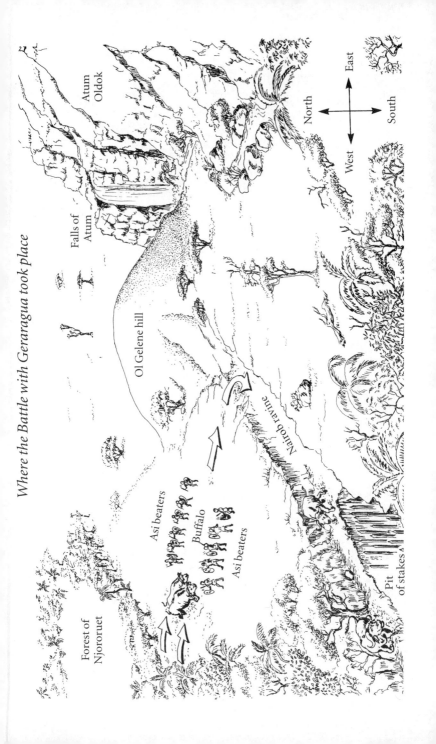

Where the Battle with Gerragua took place

Atum
Oldok

North
East
West
South

Falls of
Atum

Ol Gelene hill

Forest of
Njororuet

Asi beaters

Buffalo

Asi beaters

Nairob ravine

Pit
of stakes

1   A dark wind over the plains

'Greet the Morning Star, my son!' Tajewo lifted his small son onto his shoulder and raised his hand to the eastern sky. 'Before a man speaks to his cattle, he turns to the Morning Star, hanging there, where the sun will rise. Your father's fathers have done so since the beginning.'

They stood in the cool hour of dawn and gazed at the summit of Oldoinyo Oibor hovering above the horizon like the wings of a great white bird. 'See the wings of Kibo?' Tajewo whispered. 'Kibo is companion to the star, little one. He is a Great One of the sky. I wonder, sometimes, Lemeikoki, if the feet of a man have ever trodden his high places.'

Then Tajewo turned and strode over to the boma under the thorn trees where his cattle had sheltered overnight.

'Look, son of mine! The bull calf born to the red cow is growing fast. Watch how he butts the udder. When he is grown, he'll lead a herd like his father, the white bull. The speckled cow will drop her calf in two days, you'll see. Note them carefully, Lemeikoki, they will be yours too one day.'

Lemeikoki kicked his heels joyfully and his father steadied him lest he fall. Then he turned at a shout behind him. 'Tajewo – greetings! How are the herds this morning?'

Tajewo raised his right hand as Meromo came over to the boma, his little son tagging behind him with a herder's staff in his hands. 'All is well,' Tajewo answered. 'The bulls were restless last night. I came by to see if hyenas had pushed through the thorn fence.'

'Perhaps our bulls were envious of the beer drinking last

night and found revenge in waking men with aching heads in the small hours!' Meromo joked.

The two young men laughed and Tajewo looked fondly at Meromo. His old companion of the journey to the sacred mountain of Lengai had grown into a powerful man with broad shoulders and the strength to pull apart young bulls sparring. His ready humour filled the engang with warmth and gaiety and made him loved by all.

Tajewo himself had grown more thoughtful with the years. On their return from Lengai they had undergone their initiation ceremonies and joined the warriors of the clan. They had rejoiced in the hardships and triumphs of the warrior life. So swift was their running that their cloaks spread behind them like wings and they were called the hawks of Narokem. Their spears flew after marauding lion and the herds grazed in peace.

As foretold, Tajewo had taken the role of Alaunoni, leader of the young men. The burden of leadership had made him stand apart and look into the distance, aware of things that hardly troubled his companions. He knew that one day in the far future he would be called to speak with the spirits and to listen to voices that were only whispers to others. As time passed he grew glad of Meromo's strength and good sense.

The seasons flew by and younger men began to tread closely on their heels. Tajewo and his age mates passed through the gateway of Enuoto, the rituals of full man-hood. They wept as the long red plaits of warriorhood were shaved from their heads. They called upon the warriors of the new age set to defend them while they stood and pledged themselves by water, wood and stone to the raising of children and herds. And now, as new fathers, nothing was closer to their hearts than their families and their beautiful cattle.

'A lion – a great lion! Huger than any lion before!' shouted a boy, his feet thudding as he ran up to the boma.

'Ho, Tepilit! Brother's son! Have you woken up yet or are you still dreaming?' Meromo teased.

'It's true. Come and see!' Tepilit's chest was heaving with excitement.

The men smiled indulgently. All the same, they followed him through an opening in the thorn fence and over the grassy plain to a shallow donga. Here in the damp red earth were the prints of a huge creature.

'Eh, woh!' Meromo bent and stared. 'This was no lion,' he said, 'this was a leopard.'

'But it's too big!' cried Tepilit. 'Only a lion can be that big.'

'No, child. Look – the pug of a leopard is broader, the toes rounder and closer to the heart. This is a leopard.' Meromo stretched his hand over the spoor. 'A leopard bigger than any I've ever seen ...'

'This is what roused the cattle in the night,' said Tajewo. 'The beast that made these prints is twice the size of a maned lion. Look ... the trail leads west towards the Narok hills. Tepilit, tell the herders not to lead the cattle out this way. Let them graze east towards the river. Once a leopard has circled a village, it always returns. We must seek out this creature before it falls on our cattle.'

They stood up and walked swiftly back to the engang. 'Kidoni!' Meromo called in the direction of his brother's enclosure. 'Snatch up your spear, brother – we go out on the trail of a leopard today.'

The sun was scarcely as high as the thorn trees when Tajewo with his brother, Naikosiai, Meromo and Kidoni set out, followed by the curl-tailed dog, Moipu, to track the great leopard that had circled the village in the night.

They followed the spoor west towards the Narok hills.

All morning they ran over the grassy plains of the Narokem which spread between the Narok hills and the wide river of Naramuru in the east. The spoor was clear in the earth for there had been rain two days before. At last the leopard's tracks led into a winding gorge between the hills. Then they vanished under a tree at the foot of a krans. The men scaled the krans but when they reached the summit there was no sign of the leopard among the tumbled rocks and wind-blown trees.

'This beast is not only enormous but cunning as well,' muttered Naikosiai, sitting down wearily in the scanty shade of a tree. 'We'll walk forever over the hilltops before we find it.'

'I'm parched,' said Meromo. 'Reach me the water gourd, Kidoni. The water will make a hissing sound when it touches my throat, but I shall risk it all the same!'

They passed the gourd between them and lay back in the shade. Only Meromo prowled restlessly, still searching in vain for the spoor. Suddenly he stood still and gazed across the plains that shivered in the heat. A movement on the horizon had caught his eye. Something... was it a shadow? ... was rising slowly into the sky. Was it the smoke of a fire – or was it a storm cloud? It seemed to be growing, moving, reaching out over the plains.

'Brothers!' he called. 'Look!' His urgent pointing brought them to their feet. They shaded their eyes and stared at the horizon.

'A great burning, I think,' said Kidoni.

'No fire can move so fast,' said Naikosiai. 'It grows in size every time I blink.'

'It's a whirlwind, if I'm not mistaken,' said Tajewo. 'It cannot be anything else.'

'It's moving out of the east, spreading like a great hand

... reaching out over the plain. What if our engang lies in its path?' muttered Meromo.

'Wings of Engai!' whispered Tajewo. 'Let us get home quickly!'

They ran down from the hills and out over the plains with the speed of desperation, but long before they reached the engang, the sky grew dark and the screaming wind caught them and tossed them into the air and then dashed them to the ground whilst all around and over them flew trees and bushes. Stunned, they sprawled in the dust, unable to move, while from far off they heard the screams of women and children and the bellowing of cattle. Yet they could no more rise to help their people than a fly can crawl against a river torrent. At last the wind sank to rest and a strange silence fell over the world. Battered and bleeding, half-blind with dust, they groped for their spears; then they staggered to their feet and ran towards the engang.

They stumbled through scattered thorn branches into a scene of desolation – the boma was torn apart, their huts lay cracked open like shattered pots and every living soul had disappeared.

'Loiyan, Lemeikoki!' Tajewo tugged at the fallen mud walls of his house, but found no sign of his wife or son.

'They're gone – every one of them!' Meromo came stumbling out of his broken home. Soon Naikosiai and Kidoni came back from their empty enclosures and the four men stood staring about them, dazed with horror.

'I heard their voices in the air,' said Tajewo, 'like birds crying. Maybe the wind has carried them away over the plain and thrown them to the ground. Many will be wounded. We must find them before it is too late.'

They left their shattered homesteads and stood for a moment looking east. For as far as they could see, there was desolation. Huge thorn trees were scattered like mushrooms over the flattened grasses. Here and there the broken body of a bird lay dashed on the ground. Of their kinsfolk there was no sign. No living thing moved on the plains of Narokem.

They followed the swathe of destruction, calling the names of their families, but no answering cries came. At last, as twilight fell, Tajewo halted. The four men, tired beyond belief, stood and looked grimly over the darkening plain. 'Brothers,' said Tajewo, 'we shall soon be walking on our knees from weariness. We must stop and rest. We shall sit and take counsel before we sleep.'

Meromo remembered his firesticks in the pouch round his neck and soon he had kindled a small fire. Stiffly they sat and stared into the little flames until the breathlessness of running had passed. Tajewo spoke first. 'The spoor of a leopard that leads us away to the hills ... a leopard greater than any we've ever known ... a dark wind out of the east that carries away our people and herds while we cannot defend them ... leaving none dead on the plains, not even a lamb. There is something strange behind this, brothers ...'

Naikosiai shivered, 'It's as if the arm of an enemy has reached out and taken everything dear to us. Like a knife that cuts the heart out of a living beast. Yet whom have we offended?'

'We haven't made war on the tribes to the north for three generations,' said Tajewo.

'We haven't failed to sacrifice to the shades who plead for us in the presence of Engai,' Meromo added.

'There has been no injustice between us and those who live along the shores of the Naramuru,' said Tajewo, 'and the blood feud between us was settled before Ilkisirat.'

Just then Kidoni fell asleep where he sat and Meromo

saved him from falling into the fire in the nick of time. 'Brothers,' he said, 'we need to rest. Whatever it is that has reached out to harm us, we can do nothing now. Let's sleep and forget a little while and the dawn will lighten our minds.' With a long-drawn yawn he groaned and wrapped himself in his cloak and slept.

'Good counsel,' muttered Tajewo and within a moment or two they all lay sleeping while only the dog Moipu sat with his ears pricked beside them staring into the night.

Once, in the middle of the night the crying of a bird woke Tajewo. 'Loiyan?' he called, sitting up. But the bird cried again and he knew it was only a plover that had woken him. But the face of his wife seemed to hover before him. Where was Loiyan and where was his Lemeikoki? He thought back to the time he had first seen his beautiful wife, when he and Meromo had sheltered with her family on the way to Lengai. He remembered their courtship when messages flew like bees between their clans, and the joyous wedding feast that had made Loiyan his wife and Nandi the wife of Meromo. He thought of the children they had borne with such pride for the clan … 'Engai,' he whispered, 'look on them with mercy, shelter them beneath your wings!' Then he slept again.

They did not wake until the rays of the rising sun stung their faces and they sat up stiffly and stared around them at the plains where the only sign of life was a tiny lark rising over the bruised grasses.

'Well?' Meromo looked at Tajewo, 'Do we follow on their trail into the east, brothers?'

Tajewo stared thoughtfully at the ashes of the fire and then shook his head. 'Whoever has taken our kin has the power of a whirlwind in his hands. We are too small to fight him alone. We need the power of wisdom before we know which way to go. I think we should turn and head for the hills of Kasithi and speak with our Laibon. Only Sirigashi can see what we need to see now.'

'You're right,' said Naikosiai. 'Running before you look spears no buck, brothers. Let's go to Sirigashi.'

They gathered their gear, drank the last drops of water from their gourds and then headed away north towards the rugged blue outline of the Kasithi hills. By midday they had reached the foothills and they took a winding path uphill to the engang of Nelion, eldest son of the Laibon. Presently they were spied by a small boy perched on a rock and as they entered the enclosure Nelion's people came crowding round them. 'Brothers of Narokem, why are you bleeding? Who has been throwing stones at you and dust?'

Nelion himself, taller than them all by a head, strode forward and grasped their forearms. 'Kinsmen,' he said, 'welcome. These men need water, not words!' he called out and the long gourds resting against the walls of their huts were set before them. The four men sank down gratefully in the shade and drank the cool water. Then they told Nelion of the dark wind that had ravaged their engang. Nelion looked grave. He rose and took his staff from his hut wall. 'I'll go up to where the Old One muses among the eagles,' he said. 'Rest and wash your wounds. I'll not be long.'

But he was gone longer than was comfortable for the anxious group. They had washed the dust from their bodies and the many unnoticed wounds from flying stones were salved for them by gentle and willing hands. They had eaten and drunk again and they sat waiting still for Nelion to lead them up to counsel with the old Laibon.

Meromo kept fingering his spear. 'This waiting irks me,' he muttered. 'What if our people are being driven further and further away? How will we ever catch up with them if we spend the day sitting here?'

But Tajewo shook his head. 'How will running help us if we don't know what we are running into? He who wishes to catch a lion takes a cub as bait. We may well be walking into a trap if we follow blindly where our kin are gone.'

'Besides,' argued Naikosiai, 'who has ever consulted Sirigashi and had to walk in darkness? He is the keeper of our wisdom, remembering what goes back many lives of men, to the time when our people came out of the north. It is Sirigashi who has stored for us the knowledge of how Maitumbe and Naiterogop left the garden of God because of the serpent. It is he who tells how the great flood swept away all people and how Ol Dirima received the laws on the mountain top and how Musana declared the seventh day as a holy day, the Olon Ensubat which is sacred to Engai.'

'Ah, here comes Nelion at last!' Kidoni rose to his feet as the tall son of the Laibon strode into the enclosure. 'Surely, now we shall have a glimmer of light in this dark maze.'

'My father invites you to come and sit in council with him,' said Nelion. He led them up the hill to where, on the summit, Sirigashi withdrew to be alone. The old man sitting alone on a stone was half blind with age and yet they knew that, in the things of the spirit, his milky eyes saw further than other men did. As they came and knelt before him he reached out and took their hands, naming each of them as a father welcomes his sons. 'Sons of Narokem,' he said, 'tell me everything, from the beginning to the end and leave out nothing. Sit, my sons, and tell me of this grief.'

As they told the story of the leopard whose prints were greater than the greatest lion's, a frown grew on Sirigashi's forehead and Tajewo, who was closest to him, thought he heard him mutter that the leopard, if they had seen it, would have been as black as night and as elusive as mist. As they recounted how the dark wind had come out of the eastern plains the Laibon nodded grimly and held up his hand. 'My sons, you have told me enough. Go and rest awhile under the fig tree over there. I must speak with the shades.'

As if a load had fallen from their shoulders, they slept until Nelion woke them and told them that the Laibon was waiting for them. Sirigashi had taken his gourd of smooth river pebbles and tossed them out over a soft white hide. His old eyes could still dimly tell the white from the black and grey and his hands had fumbled softly over the stones, turning them this way and that until his spirit found the still point in which he could hear what spirit voices told him. As Tajewo and his brothers approached, he rose to his feet and, leaning on his staff, he said, 'My sons, it is well you have come to me. I have heard from the shades who watch over us. Three things I have heard. The first is the story of two young boys crossing a river on their way to the sacred mountain, Lengai. They told me also of a beautiful woman praying beside a sacred fig tree, sorrowing for the lack of a child. The third thing of which they spoke is a stone, as clear as water in sunlight.' The seer fell silent and stared at them with penetration before he said, 'Tell me, to whom do these things belong?'

'Surely the boys who crossed the river of Ndamathia were Meromo and myself,' said Tajewo and then he was silent remembering the time when his beautiful Loiyan had watched Nandi bear two children while she longed in vain for a baby at her breast. She had wandered far, as barren wives do, to holy places to pray. 'Perhaps the sorrowing woman was Loiyan, though how could evil have come of her prayers?' he pondered. 'But I know nothing of a stone.'

Sirigashi sighed. 'What has happened now is like a tree with its roots in another time. You must go into the east, Tajewo, to retrieve your kin and your herds.'

'But who has taken them?' cried Meromo. 'Who is our enemy and why?'

'My son,' said Sirigashi, 'these things will be revealed as you journey east. It is best that you see only as far as the next step. I shall bless you before I send you out against a powerful foe. Tread warily for you take a path into great danger. You, Tajewo and Meromo, must be the spearhead, for, whether you willed it or not, it is from your past deeds that this trouble has come. Remember that you face one who is crooked in his ways, therefore your defence is in purity of heart. Do nothing alone and accept help that comes from humble and unexpected places. There is a stone at the centre of this and in its heart I saw light. The moon will rise soon and lighten your path into the eastern plains. Go swiftly, my sons, and may the wings of Engai shelter you.' He reached out to bless them. Then he sent them down the hill in the blue dusk. Nelion's wives ran out with gifts of cheese and water and Nelion himself accompanied them down to the foothills. 'Go under the wings, brothers of Narokem, we are mindful of you. Our warriors' arms will be yours at the word.'

They thanked Nelion and then they turned east to face the rising moon. They ran for many hours until the stars began to fade and then they stopped to rest under a thorn tree. Kidoni and Naikosiai fell asleep the moment their heads touched their folded arms, but Meromo heard Tajewo turn restlessly and sigh. 'Heart's brother,' he said, 'what keeps you awake?'

'It's the thought that something I have done has caused this disaster,' muttered Tajewo. 'How easy it is for a small thing to grow into a great one.'

'If it is indeed something to do with the journey to Lengai,' said Meromo, 'then I am in it just as deep as you are. I shall never leave you to take the punishment alone.'

'I have the truest friend a man can have,' Tajewo reached out and gripped Meromo's arm. 'And look at Moipu. He will sit beside us, alert and watchful till sunrise and we need not fear wild dogs or lion because he is with us. Together we may find our way out of this dark adventure.'

'How my bones ache,' murmured Meromo. 'Sleep now and rest your thoughts, warrior, otherwise our feet will stumble on the path tomorrow.'

At last they slept while the faithful Moipu kept watch under the stars.

2   Moloch of Lolmoloch

Kidoni woke first, at sunrise and shook his companions awake. They rose and took up their spears and then ran steadily towards the rising sun. Suddenly, at midday, Meromo stopped with a cry of surprise and picked up a necklet of blue and red beads. 'My mother gave this to Nandi two moons ago,' he said, 'there can be no doubt that our people have passed this way.'

For two days they journeyed, resting very little and eating even less, running with long measured strides as only the plainsmen can run. On the morning of the third day the hills of Naramuru loomed against the eastern sky and they ran on until at dusk the trail led them into a narrow valley between the hills.

'Look!' Meromo, who was in the lead, had come upon a swathe of damp sand, deeply churned by cattle. And over the hoof prints were the footprints of women and children.

'Ha!' Kidoni squatted to point at footprints along the edge of the trail. 'My old father came limping along here. I'd know his left foot with the missing toe anywhere. And here is my wife – carrying Mokot, for her footprints press deep into the sand. Thanks be to Engai – they were alive when they reached this place.'

They passed along the valley between fever trees glimmering gold in the evening light and suddenly they found themselves on the bank of a wide river. On the far side loomed dark kranses and beyond them the forested foothills of Oldoinyo Oibor rose in black waves to touch the first stars. Moipu ran along the river bank and then sat on his haunches and gave a long, quivering howl. The men shivered and drew their cloaks round them as a cold white mist came floating down the valley.

Tajewo gripped his spear. 'This is a strange place, brothers. I sense a presence brooding here – as if someone is watching us.' They glanced around anxiously but all they could see was the mist creeping over the water and rising up against the black kranses.

It was Meromo who shook himself free of the sense of dread. 'If we have to spend the night in this cold hole we'd better find firewood before darkness falls.'

They found a sheltered hollow beside an outcrop of rock, still warm from the sun and presently Meromo and Kidoni had collected dry grass and driftwood and kindled a small fire. They huddled round it and shared the last of their cheese.

'This place has an evil feel to it,' said Meromo. 'We should keep watch. I'll take the first hours. Sleep, my brothers.' Leaning against his spear he sat on the boulders above them while his grateful companions rolled themselves in their cloaks and fell asleep. He fed the fire with wood and stared into the mist, for he could not shake off the sense of watching eyes. Yet all he saw was the mist that moved like a living creature through the valley. He woke Naikosiai who kept watch until the middle of the night and then woke Kidoni. He too sat through the silent hours and woke Tajewo for the last watch.

Tajewo's limbs were stiff with sleep and he paced along the river bank, bending now and then to search for driftwood with which to enliven the dying embers. A chill wind began to whisper through the trees and he stood and listened. Was it the wind's voice sighing, as if a great cloak had swirled over the black kranses? Or had someone called his name? Tajewo froze and waited, drawing his cloak about him and grasping his spear shaft. Then from the rocks that loomed above the mist came a hollow whisper: 'Tajewo!'

A cold breeze came eddying over the water and extinguished the flames of the fire: 'Tajewo!'

Tajewo stepped up on a boulder on the river bank and cried, 'I am here! Who calls me?'

'You may well ask, Tajewo of the Narokem. I am Moloch of the Lolmoloch River and I have summoned you, arrogant one of the plains, to pay for a wrong you have done me. Many years have passed since you insulted and injured my son, Ndamathia, and I have waited in vain for a sacrifice of propitiation. Now I have claimed your people and your cattle in recompense.'

So that was it. Tajewo hung his head in dismay for Moloch spoke the truth. On their way to Lengai, he and Meromo had crossed the river in which the monster Ndamathia lurked. In their haste, they had forgotten to cast a gift into the water and Ndamathia had risen angrily to take them as his prey. If it hadn't been for the charm bird, Entirritirri, who had flown and pecked at Ndamathia's eyes, the boys would never have reached Lengai.

'Great One,' said Tajewo, 'in the ignorance of youth, I did indeed neglect to make a crossing gift to Ndamathia. But drought was eating up our people and we were travelling in haste to Lengai to seek the rain charm of the seer, Natana Ole Kerewa. Is it nothing to you, Moloch, that we underwent trials and hardship and set free the charm that brought back the rain? Was the rain that nourished the dry river beds not recompense for the thoughtless act of an uncircumcised boy?'

'The rain has not washed away the injury to Ndamathia,'

Moloch answered. 'And I never forget an insult. Therefore, Tajewo, I have taken your people and your cattle. Each day from this rock of Lolgoron I shall cast a sacrifice for Ndamathia.'

Tajewo's heart turned cold and he felt the anguish of guilt. He was a man of wisdom and had often listened to the council of elders. He knew that the law of his people, the law upheld by Sirigashi, demanded recompense for his offence against Ndamathia. He, Tajewo, had brought Moloch's anger on his people and he must pay the price. As they do at a council of war, he struck his spear shaft on the stone and called out, 'I am indeed to blame, Moloch of Lolmoloch. I neglected the river offering and it is through me that Ndamathia was insulted. Name the number of cattle you desire in recompense and I shall drive them to the banks of Lolmoloch. I shall cast the libation of enkiroret upon the water as a peace offering. Let me pay the customary price, Moloch, and release my kin.'

But Moloch answered with chilling mockery: 'No offering of milk and honey is as sweet to me as revenge. I wish to indulge my children who lurk in the deep pools and tomorrow as the sun rises the first sacrifice will be thrown from the rock of Lolgoron.'

'Let me be the sacrifice, then!' Tajewo cried. 'The fault is mine and I am willing to pay for it with my life!'

Now Tajewo knew with whom he was dealing. The name of Moloch was a byword for evil among those who lived on the plains and foothills of Oldoinyo Oibor. He was an ancient and powerful spirit who lived in the caverns of Lolgoron and who roamed the river banks, driven by a hunger that was never appeased. Young girls who came to the river to fetch water never returned home and his dark servants, the crocodiles, dragged children and calves to their lonely deaths. One still evening as he brooded among the kranses of the river, he had seen a young woman, beautiful in spite of the tears on her dusty cheeks. She had gathered grasses by the river, which she had laid in the fork of a sacred fig tree. Then she had leaned her head on her hands and prayed: 'Lengai, Mother of Goodness, hear me. I wander alone. In danger I travel from one horizon to the other. I beseech you, Lengai, you whose wings shine as the rainbow – give me a child. You who are a mother, grant me motherhood, that I may stay contented at home, as other women do.'

To Moloch, watching, it had seemed then that the rays of the setting sun shone among the leaves of the fig tree with the brilliance of many-coloured wings. He had turned away from the brightness to the black rocks of the river. The woman with tears on her cheeks had slept curled in her cloak under the sacred tree and when the first birds called, she was gone. Thwarted, Moloch had returned to the caverns of Lolgoron, but the memory of the woman had gnawed at him and in time he had learned from his spies that she was the beloved of Tajewo.

Moloch was silent. Tajewo's self-offering was a thing he had not bargained for. Moloch had never loved a living thing and he was puzzled by a man who would willingly give up his life so that his kin might live. He laughed contemptuously. 'What pleasure would Ndamathia find in the bones of one thin man! However, I have a mind to accept a gift of cattle. But instead of your life, I demand the woman Loiyan.'

Tajewo was struck dumb, wrestling with the anguish in his heart. How could he send his kin to their deaths in order to save Loiyan? She would not wish them to die so that she might live, for she loved every one of them as much as herself. What would the wise Sirigashi judge in a case like this? Presently it came to him that Loiyan herself should be the one to choose her fate.

'Moloch of Lolmoloch!' he called. 'Hear me! Call my wife, Loiyan, and let her be the judge of what she will do! She is not my water pot or my sleeping mat to do with as I please.'

Again Moloch was silent. It was very strange to him that this puny being who owned a woman should wish to set her free to fly like a bird where she chose. Moloch knew only the pleasure of power and possession; the love that sets free had never grown in his heart. Assuredly, he mused, this Tajewo was a creature of weak wits. Yet ... he showed a certain courage ... If he were prepared to sacrifice himself for the safety of his people, would he not perhaps be willing to accomplish other feats? To undertake some dangerous and unpleasant task...? A long-cherished hope rose in Moloch's mind. Surely he could put this little weakling to some use before he devoured him and his kin?

'There is one thing that I shall accept in the place of your people, Tajewo,' he said. 'One thing only. It is the Stone of Naiterogop. Bring the stone here to me, on the rock of Lolgoron, on the night when the new moon first hangs in the sky. If you fail, your people will die and I shall take the woman Loiyan for myself.'

Moloch's voice faded among the kranses and Tajewo stood dumb with despair. As he turned and stepped down from the rock he found his three companions standing there, clutching their spears, staring into the mist.

'So,' Meromo spat into the sand angrily, 'it is Moloch, the old demon, whose greed has drawn us across the plains. He is exacting a heavy penalty for the mistake of an uncircumcised boy. Always the sign of a bully.'

'You spoke well, brother,' said Naikosiai. 'As a warrior

should, taking the danger on your own shoulders.'

'But what is the Stone of Naiterogop?' asked Tajewo.

'I've never heard of it,' said Meromo and the others shook their heads. 'Naiterogop, Mother of us all, we know, but the old tales say nothing of a stone.'

'Old scorpion!' Meromo hissed scornfully and then squatted beside the fire to coax up flames with scraps of kindling. The stars were fading and he was feeling the pangs of hunger. When the fire was crackling again he disappeared into the mist and came back shortly with two mudfish which he roasted and broke for his companions. Presently the sun rose and the mist lifted. They ate in silence, frowning a little as they searched their memories for some clue as to the Stone of Naiterogop.

'The old devil means to devour us, that's clear,' growled Naikosiai. 'First we have to find a stone we know nothing of – neither what it is nor where it can be found – and, since the moon is just after the full, we have only twenty days in which to find it.'

'Find it we must, my brother,' said Tajewo, rising stiffly. 'Or we lose all we hold dear in this world.'

They gathered up their gear and stood looking across the river to the black basalt krans of Lolgoron. Below it, in the still green water the backs of crocodiles glided slowly. A sense of foreboding gripped them and it crossed their minds that their quest for an unknown stone was sure to end in the depths of the Lolmoloch in the jaws of Moloch's creatures. For Moloch's power was everywhere. It brooded over the black kranses and drifted in the chill air around them and they knew themselves to be small and helpless in the thrall of his malice.

A volley of excited barks broke into the spell of Lolgoron. Moipu was running in circles over the river bank. He trotted up to Tajewo and whined and then ran away to the water's edge before he paused and wagged his tail, as if inviting them to follow. Then he leaped out onto a rocky spit that ran into the river. Once more he turned and looked back at his master. Then he sprang over the narrow channel between the rocks and a sandbank on the far shore, and disappeared behind tumbled boulders. Presently they saw him trotting along a path up the hillside, his nose to the ground.

'What has your hunter of bush cats found now?' muttered Meromo.

'It must be the spoor left by our kin,' said Tajewo. 'Come, let's follow him,' and he strode off along the river bank and sprang out over the rocks across the river. His companions came close on his heels and soon they found the path up the hillside where Moipu stood waiting for them. It was a narrow path between huge boulders, winding into the rocky foothills of the mountain.

Presently the path forked. The left fork led down into a valley and here in the muddy ground they found the spoor of their people and cattle again. The right hand fork led on up the hill into thick forest. Moipu sat on this path, wagging his tail, with his tongue hanging out.

Tajewo hesitated a moment. 'The left path is where our people have gone. Why doesn't Moipu take that trail?'

'Never mind that rat-catcher,' said Naikosiai. 'We must find our families. Come on!' He hastened down the left path into a narrow valley, following the spoor of cattle and kinsfolk. The others followed him until they came to a narrow pass between two kranses. Suddenly Naikosiai stopped in his tracks and Meromo bumped into him, stubbing his toes. 'What –?'

'Shh!' Naikosiai pointed at a glint of light among the trees ahead.

'Men down there – with spears!' he whispered. 'Moloch is guarding his prey.'

'At least it is a sign that they are still alive, as he claims,' said Kidoni. 'But we would be fools to approach. We must go back before we are seen.' In silence they retraced their steps to where the paths forked.

Moipu was still sitting, scratching himself placidly, as if all along he had known the way they should go. 'This time we shall follow our humble servant and see where this path leads us,' said Tajewo. 'Show us the way, great one, and we shall follow you.' Moipu trotted up a steep, forested foothill that reached down from the great mountain to the crags of Lolmoloch. Somewhere among the trees a stream was chuckling and mist, golden in the sunlight, came floating between the leaves. The path went up and up, twisting under tall ironwoods and all the while the mist flowed around them in a soft golden cloud.

At last the path ended at the mouth of a cave from which the mist was flowing, like water from a fountain. Somewhere deep inside someone was singing a quavering song in a language that was strange to them and yet, somehow, familiar too. Moipu hopped onto the rocky ledge at the cave mouth and sat wagging his tail and barking as if he expected to be received there as an old friend. There was a clatter of pots and gourds and a cracked old voice grumbled plaintively. Moipu answered it with an eager whine and two sharp barks. From the cavern a listening silence was followed by shuffling sounds. Again Moipu called and a moment later the mist parted and the strange and wrinkled face of an ancient woman peered out at them.

She came forward, shading her eyes against the sunlight. 'Men!' The aged face screwed itself into an angry scowl. She raised a carved pole and brandished it. 'Get away from here! I'll not have Moloch's spies nosing round my cave. Don't think I'm blind to your trickery. There's wickedness afoot, dark and crooked doings – I know, oh, I know! You may tell your master I'm not afraid of him. Go back to your nasty holes under Lolgoron and leave me alone. Go on – be off with you!'

The old creature disappeared into the curtain of mist and presently great billows of white fog rolled down from the cavern like smoke from the pipe of an angry elder. The men were dumbfounded but Moipu was not cowed by the tirade and in that ancient language which is shared by living creatures and the Keepers of Forest, Mist and Mountain, he spoke to the old woman again. At last the sound of stirring within the cavern ceased and once more the crone emerged and listened to Moipu while she stared with penetrating golden eyes at Tajewo and his companions.

In astonishment they gazed back at her. Her long, white hair was as wild as the moss on mountain trees. She wore a cloak of colobus skins in which small creatures clung, while a dwarf mongoose lay curled asleep round her neck. Over her bosom and shoulders the seeds of trees were sprouting, a tribe of suricates swarmed over her feet and from her ear-lobe hung a small bat.

She looked them up and down and muttered to herself, as if recollecting old, half-remembered things: 'By the stones of Weru,' she murmured, 'these are tall, thin ones. The dog is right. These are not Moloch's servants, they are plainsmen. It has been a long time since I saw any of those. Yes, indeed, plainsmen they are!' She shuffled forward and leaned on her staff while her strange golden eyes regarded them curiously. 'Well,' she said at last, 'tall travellers, what brings you to the cavern of Marumuruti?'

Tajewo stepped forward and saluted her courteously. 'We

come from the Narokem in the west, Old Mother,' he answered. 'We have come in search of our people who have been swept away in a whirlwind and hidden by Moloch. He has taken them as payment for a transgression I committed many years ago at the river of Ndamathia.'

As he spoke, Marumuruti's eyes widened. She glanced round and whispered conspiratorially, 'Aaaaaah. So! You are enemies of Moloch, are you? Well, then you are undoubtedly friends of mine. Come in!' She beckoned to them. 'Come inside and let us talk together!'

3 The Mother of Mists' story

Beyond the curtain of mist, Marumuruti's cavern yawned dark and deep, reaching through unseen passages into the mountain. Everywhere, through crevices and fissures, the roots of trees reached long grey fingers that seemed to move in the flickering firelight. Between the roots small creatures crept and scuttled. Eyes glinted and tails whisked and everywhere there was scuffling and the scratch of small claws. The water in the cauldron seethed and bubbled and sang to itself and, like everything else in Marumuruti's cavern, it seemed to be more than usually alive.

'There is magic here,' whispered Meromo.

'Good magic, surely,' Tajewo murmured. 'Look at that dog of mine. He sits and watches the old one as if she had fed him all his life.'

But Naikosiai caught sight of an owl perched in a corner and gripped Tajewo's arm. 'I fear we have to do with a witch – the owl up there gives her away.'

The four men stared at the owl which blinked its golden eyes and stared back unafraid. Meanwhile Marumuruti was busy piling grass against the cavern wall. She patted it invitingly: 'Come and rest yourselves, men of Narokem. You've travelled far and before you tell me your story, you must drink a little beer to refresh yourselves.' But she turned to find her guests transfixed with fear, staring first at the owl and then at her, as if they expected to be turned into beetles at any moment. Marumuruti straightened up. 'Ah, I see,' she said. 'You have seen Kovankuni, and you take me for a witch. No, sons of Narokem, I am no witch, though I do not blame you for thinking so. You have never met a Keeper before, though you may have heard of us in fireside tales and thought we were only the imaginings of grandmothers.' As she looked at each of them with her penetrating golden eyes they knew that the powers of the old woman were very deep but that goodness flowed from her as water from a fountain. 'I, Marumuruti, am older than any witch – I am older than many lives of men or women and I speak the language long forgotten by humankind – the language of forest and river and all living things. I am Keeper of the river valleys. The mists of Marumuruti nourish the forests and the river banks, even in driest years. All creatures are my friends – except for those few whom Moloch has perverted to his ends. Do not fear my Kovankuni for she is my eyes and ears. You will have need of her wisdom and her silent flight. And do not be afraid of me, for I am a mother to all who love the world which Engai shelters. Now, sit down and share my honey beer.'

Fear changed to wonder as the plainsmen sank into the sweet grass and accepted the welcome pot she held out to them. Then Marumuruti took up her staff and went over to the cauldron. 'Presently you shall tell me your story, but first I shall draw up the mist to hide us. Moloch's spies creep even to the threshold of my cavern these days.'

She plunged her wooden staff deep into the cauldron and began to stir. As she stirred she began to sing and the mist billowed up thick and white until it hid them from the world. And the singing of Marumuruti, a low humming sound, like a nest of bees in a hollow tree, loosened their weary limbs and they slept. Only Moipu remained awake, his nose pointing towards the cauldron, sniffing the falling mist and feeling the strength of the old singer flowing into him along nose and paws until it rose into the tips of his hair and his tail and sent him dancing and spinning across the cavern.

When the singing and stirring were done, Marumuruti wove a binding spell upon the mist, to hold it close around them. Then she poked the sleeping men awake with her staff. 'Now, warriors,' she said, 'no one but ourselves will hear what we have to say. Remember – Moloch has his minions. Beware of the mottled horsefly, of Mzinzi, the black crake, and the black and yellow water snake for they go hither and thither with tales.' Marumuruti sat down on a carved wooden chair and fixed her eyes on them. 'Begin at the beginning and tell me everything that has happened to bring you here. And don't leave anything out. There is nothing I dislike more than a story half told, not so, my Kovankuni?' The owl hooted and ducked in agreement and the old woman settled to listen.

Then Tajewo told her of the journey to the summit of Lengai, to find Natana Ole Kerewa, the keeper of the rain charm. He told her how they had completed the tasks that Natana had set them and how the rain charm had swept out from Lengai bringing the life-restoring rain.

Marumuruti listened carefully, nodding now and then. Then she frowned and said, 'Tell me again of the river crossing.'

Then Meromo recounted how they had forgotten to throw a gift to Ndamathia when they had crossed his river and how he had risen in anger and claimed their lives, and how the bird Entirritirri had saved them by pecking at his eyes.

'To neglect the gift of the river crossing was indeed a discourtesy – a grave mistake,' said Marumuruti. 'But you were young and uncircumcised. Such an error should be forgiven a boy and should not be a killing matter. Indeed the lord of the Lolmoloch had reason to forgive a rain bringer, for his children too are nourished by rain. But Moloch's heart is dark and his mind spins cunning webs.'

'Old Mother, what is this Stone of Naiterogop that Moloch desires?' asked Meromo.

'That I can tell you,' muttered Marumuruti. 'But it is a long tale and since you are men and have come far, you are sure to be hungry before I am halfway through. Let me bring you something to eat and then I shall not be interrupted by the rumbling of empty stomachs!' Marumuruti heaved herself to her feet and brought them cheese and sour red berries from the forest. Then she made herself comfortable again and prodded Moipu who lay sleeping at her feet. 'You have a wise little servant, men of the plains, for he has led you to one who can help you. As you have listened to him, listen to my tale. Now, when you sat beside your grand-mothers' hearth fires, did you not hear of Naiterogop, the first mother and Maitumbe, the first father?'

'Yes, indeed,' said Naikosiai. 'We know of the old ones, shaped by the hands of God and given the care of the gar-den of Paradise. But we were never told of a stone.'

'Perhaps storytellers are not what they were,' muttered Marumuruti. 'But where your grandmothers have failed, I shall fill the pot. Now listen and, little by little, it will become clear to you. Everyone knows how God made the first man, Maitumbe, and the first woman, Naiterogop, and how He set them down in the garden of Paradise where the rain never failed and the trees gave fruit always. In Paradise there was no pain and no sorrow. The man and woman wore no clothes, for the sun shone gently over them and the cold never pinched them. And God used to come down from the sky on a shining ladder to visit His children. He would sit at their hearth fire as one friend visits another.'

Marumuruti paused and sighed. 'But there was a tree, yes, there was one tree alone which bore fruit that was a delight to the eyes. They might eat the fruit of all other trees, said the Lord God, but not of that tree. At first they used to walk a long way round the tree.

'Now, one day the three-headed serpent came and twined himself round that forbidden tree and he watched Naiterogop as she walked in the garden alone. And the serpent saw how she stood afar and looked at the forbidden tree and wondered. Yes, she was wondering about the tree that God had made tabu. And the serpent was old and knowing. "Ah, Naiterogop!" he said, drawing her closer with his whispering, "can it be true, what I hear? Can it be true that the Lord God has said you may not eat of the lovely fruit of this tree?"

'"It is true," admitted Naiterogop. "The Lord God does not wish it."

'"But you, Naiterogop, who are no less than a daughter of God, do you not wonder what it tastes like?"

'"Yes, I do," sighed Naiterogop.

'"Daughter of God," whispered the serpent, "it is said that God is almighty and all knowing. Would such a father waste His time in making a tree if He did not mean His children to eat of its fruit?"

'"I do not know," said the woman. "It seems that I know very little, after all."

'"Yet you are the daughter of the all-knowing one. Would you not like to understand everything, just as He does?"

'Naiterogop loved and admired her father God and she said, "Yes, that I would like."

'"Listen to me, then," whispered the serpent, "because I know a secret: if you take just one little bite of this fruit, you will know as much as God Himself." He slid along a branch and bent it down invitingly towards her. At the tip of the branch hung a fruit that was beautiful to see and very sweet to smell. "Come," said the serpent, "eat and grow wise, daughter of God."

'Naiterogop reached up and pulled the fruit from the tree. She tasted it and it was sweet. Quickly she plucked another fruit and ran to find Maitumbe. She held it out to him and Maitumbe looked at the juice on her chin and the wild brightness in her eyes and he took the fruit and ate it. Then, even as they swallowed the fruit, it seemed to them that the world changed around them. Their eyes saw differently. They saw that they were small and naked and needing to hide themselves. And when God came down, looking for His children, He could not find them. So patiently He went looking and at last He found them covering themselves with leaves.

'"Why are you hiding yourselves, my children?" asked the Lord God, although, you know, He could see from their eyes that they had eaten the fruit.

'"It suddenly seemed to us that we were naked," muttered Maitumbe, "and therefore we must cover ourselves."

'"Ah, my son," the Lord God asked, "what opened your eyes to your nakedness?"

'"It was the fruit," answered Maitumbe, looking at the ground for the eyes of the Lord hurt his eyes. "This woman of mine picked it and gave it to me. You know what women are."

'"Yes, I know how men are too," the Lord God smiled, then, I am sure,' muttered Marumuruti, peering over her cheeks at her listeners.

'The Lord looked at Naiterogop and His eyes hurt her, though there was no anger in them. "Beloved daughter," He began and she answered, "It was the three-headed serpent who talked me into it!"

' "I thought as much," said the Lord God. "I expect he told you that when you had eaten you would know everything there is to know." And He called to the serpent where he lay curled round the tree, pretending to be asleep, but listening to every word. He had one gloating moment of pleasure when he saw the two foolish mortals, of whom he was jealous, standing naked and ashamed before God their Father.

'The Lord God pointed His finger at the snake. "You are to leave Paradise," He said. "You'll make do in the desert from now on. You'll live in holes in the hard ground for when the sons of Naiterogop see you they will throw stones at you and kill you if they can."

'The serpent went. He went slowly and gracefully, as if he didn't care one way or the other, but he did give one regretful glance back at the soft grasses of Paradise. Then the Lord God turned to Naiterogop and Maitumbe and said, "My children, you have chosen the way of knowing and it is a stony way. The garden of Paradise can no longer be your home. You will always remember it and even your children's children will think of it with longing. Now you must take your herds and go out by the gate to the west, into the land of sorrows."

'Maitumbe and Naiterogop took their herds and left the garden of Paradise. Lest they try and return, God told the angel of the Morning Star to stand at the western gate and hold his flaming sword across it. Yes,' Marumuruti sighed, 'that's the way it was.'

Kidoni echoed her sigh. 'That's the story we remember from childhood, Old One. And still we yearn for Paradise – we, the great-great grandchildren of Naiterogop, seem to remember dimly how it was.'

'Indeed,' murmured the old woman. 'Yet this is only the beginning of the story I am going to tell,' she lowered her voice. 'This tale has been recounted by old women for as long as the daughters of Naiterogop have told stories by the hearth fire. It is a long tale – I tell it a small step at a time. Now, when Maitumbe and Naiterogop walked out of Paradise and saw the stony land before them, their hearts died. Naiterogop turned and looked back through the gate into Paradise where the grass was green and a cool breeze rustled through the fruiting trees and the perfume of white flowers sweetened the air. With her hand on her heart she wept. She wept at leaving the presence of her Father God. She wept for her children and her children's children who would never know Paradise. The Morning Star, that great angel, saw her grief. He saw that her heart was breaking, not only for herself but also for those unborn. Her sorrow touched his heart and as he held the sword across the gate he wept for her. A tear fell from his eye upon the sand of the desert and became a hard, glistening stone.

'Through her tears Naiterogop saw the tear fall and she looked up and saw the pity in the face of the angel. She picked up the stone and held it in her shaking hands. "The Morning Star has wept with me," she whispered, "I shall keep his tear always, for if he has felt my grief, will the Lord God not also grow kind again one day?"

'Several times she looked back over her shoulder as they walked into the west, into the desert and the twilight. As they went the light of the Morning Star, which is also the Evening Star, still hung in the sky. To Naiterogop his light was like a promise. The daughters of Naiterogop have looked for it ever since at twilight and dawn. Now,' the old woman paused, her eyes glistening a little at the memory of Naiterogop's sorrow, 'that stone, the tear that was shed by the Morning Star for the first mother, that stone is also called the Stone of Naiterogop.'

The curiosity on the faces of her listeners changed to awe. 'Surely no mere man could hold this stone in his hands and live!' whispered Meromo. 'The tear of an angel is a holy thing.'

'You might say so,' the old woman nodded. 'But there is holding and holding. When the stone was held with an open palm, with a generous heart, it gave good things. But when it was held in a closed fist by one who hoarded it against others, then evil came of it, as you will see.'

'The years went by, and when Naiterogop was dying she called her eldest daughter to her and gave her the stone, telling her that when she herself came to die she must leave it to her eldest daughter. And so the stone passed from the hand of a mother to her daughter for many, many lives. Only when there is no daughter does a mother give it to a son and he must give it back into the hands of his first-born daughter when she comes of age.'

The Mother of Mists paused in her narration. She went over to a pile of kindling and took up some branches of red thorn wood that she pushed into the embers under the cauldron. When the flames were licking up the sides of the pot again, she took up her staff and stirred until mist drew a thick white silence around them. Then she sat down once more and the rise and fall of her voice held them in thrall with the ancient tales she had gathered and hoarded through the years.

'Well now, the children of Maitumbe and Naiterogop grew to be as many as the stars in the night sky. And still the Stone of Naiterogop passed from mother to daughter and was kept hidden, known only to one or two, here and there. Then came a time of famine. War followed on the famine and the children of Maitumbe and Naiterogop were scattered, like dry leaves in the wind. They wandered away to the north and the south, to the east and the west. It is those who came south who made our story. They came driving their herds beside the great river through the desert and among them travelled a daughter of Naiterogop, called Bia, who was a holder of the Star's Tear. Bia married the Lion King who lived in a fortress of rock in the southern desert – there where they live in caves cut out of the high rocks, above the desert sands. Bia bore two sons and the stone passed into the hands of the elder son, Kerag. Kerag ruled after his father as Lion King and his power and fame spread very far. Yet, as his wealth grew his people dwindled for he sold them as slaves to men who came across the sea in ships.'

'Sea?' exclaimed Meromo. 'What is sea and what are ships?'

'The sea is a great lake, the greatest of all,' Marumuruti answered. 'Its water is salt like the lakes to the north where flamingos nest. But the sea stretches to the very edge of the world, so they say.' She looked at their doubting faces and chuckled. 'Ah, you men of the plains, you cannot believe it! But I have lived a long time and I've spoken with those, now and then, who have travelled very, very far. For you the world is bounded by the mountain of Lengai to the south, the plains in the west and the white wings of Kibo in the east. But there is more to the world than that – much more! East beyond Kibo stretch more plains and east beyond them lies the sea. And the sea goes on into the remote east to where the sun rises, like a bird rising from water at dawn.'

'And these ships?' muttered Meromo.

'A ship, they say, is a basket made of the wood of tall trees. It is big enough to carry many men. The basket floats upon the water and wings – sails they call them, pull it over the water. Just as the wind fills your cloak and tugs you, running, over the ground, so the breath of the wind fills the sails and they pull the ships over the sea to other lands.'

The men were silent and Marumuruti saw their bewildered glances and chuckled till the small creatures that slept in the folds of her mantle opened their eyes at the unaccustomed quivering. 'Ah,' she said, 'I do not blame you for doubting me. The mind can make only so many new pictures in one day. Now you must listen to the rest of my story and believe it if you can, for soon you will come walking into it yourselves. Well, as I was saying, Kerag the king traded people, his own people and those of nearby kingdoms whom he hunted with his bandits. He sold them for strange and beautiful woven cloth brought by men from the east and also for a bright metal, called gold – more precious than iron or copper because it does not change and is the colour of the setting sun on water. For these and for spices and coloured stones he sold them. And before you interrupt me again, I shall tell you what a slave is. You make a man a slave when you set him to work like a donkey, to carry heavy loads along the path you wish. Slavery is when you tether a man by the leg and keep him as an animal to work and live for you alone, not according to the wishes of his own heart. And his heart dies slowly within him and his will goes out like a small flame blown out by the wind. Yes, you proud men of the plains know nothing of such things, but there are those who suffer them, nonetheless.

'Now, listen well, for indeed the Stone of Naiterogop is coming closer. The Lion King Kerag had a younger brother, Agal, who was pure in heart. One night as he slept, his dead mother, Bia, came to him in a dream. She was sorrowful because of Kerag's wickedness. It grieved her spirit that the

Stone of Naiterogop should give power to one who sold his people for his own gain. She laid upon Agal the task of redeeming the tear of the Morning Star. He woke and stole into his brother's room and took the stone and his young sister and fled south into the great mountains. Generations passed and there are many tales of a people who always lived in a green place, even when drought scourged the plains and locusts darkened the sky. The stories are too many to tell you now, but it seems as if, wherever a daughter of Naiterogop held the stone that famine could not touch her people. But there came a time when drought and then plague killed the tribes and their herds. People cast envious eyes at people of the stone. They drove them out of their fertile valleys and they fled south again, scattered and persecuted until at last, upon this very mountain, a girl was seen who wore a circlet of gold round her forehead with a bright stone in it. She was pursued by evil men to the heights of Kibo. She died there, they say, and so did those who followed her.' Marumuruti fell silent and her eyes were sad.

'And where is the stone now, Old Mother?' Naikosiai asked quietly.

'I cannot be sure,' she pondered. 'There is one more story to tell and then you will know as much as I do. Kovankuni heard it from Mwere, the nightjar who is no idle gossip. That year, Tajewo, when you set free the rain charm from the summit of Lengai, that year the storms flew out over the land with a force almost forgotten by men. Thunder crashed across the heavens as the black wings of the rain-bird settled heavily upon Oldoinyo Oibor. A bright stone was washed into a mountain torrent and over the falls of Atum Oldok into the chasms below.'

'How can we ever hope to retrieve it?' Tajewo's voice was flat with disappointment. 'We are plainsmen who can hardly swim a river, let alone dive into the whirlpools below a waterfall.'

'If it lay in the whirlpool of Atum, then indeed you would have no hope,' Marumuruti replied. 'But Mwere, who crouches close to the ground and hears the talk of small creatures, heard from a wagtail, blown down from the forest, something strange that has made me wonder and wonder. In the kranses of Atum Oldok the lower cliffs are full of caves, like crab holes in a river bank. There is a tale of a great fish caught below the falls by Nsi, the otter, who was seen with a sparkling plaything in his fingers. Nsi played his fill and forgot his plaything. Ravens came for the fish-pickings and a raven flew with a bright stone to its nest in the cliffs above. Perhaps it was wind or rain that tumbled the stone from the raven's nest, but it must have fallen deep into a cave where a lizard had its lair. The stone has not been seen again, but something strange and horrible has emerged from the caverns of Atum Oldok and I have no doubt that the stone is in it somewhere.'

Suddenly, the call of a nightjar roused the old woman and she started up and peered out of the cave, shaking her head and tut-tutting. 'The telling of tales has almost put it out of my head. It is time to work now, time to fill the valleys with night mist.' She took up her staff and set to stirring her cauldron. When the clouds billowed forth she went to the mouth of her cavern and stood there singing a low song and waving her arms while the mist flowed away in a white stream. It was deep dusk and they looked out and saw the first stars hanging in the sky.

While the night mist flowed away into the river valleys, Marumuruti busied herself with a little hearth fire that burned night and day in a corner. She poked some sweet yams into the embers and raked them over. She dragged out a cooking pot and placed it on the hearthstones, adding herbs and leaves to a stew and stirring. 'I may be old and live alone, but I have not yet forgotten what hungry men wish to find in a cooking pot,' she muttered, prodding the yams that were beginning to whistle among the coals. 'There will be lean days ahead of them, no doubt – they must eat while they can.'

Before long, with a clatter of gourd bowls and ladles she was serving out stew and steaming yams. In the silence of deep gratitude the men ate their fill and then they settled back into the warmth of their cloaks and the mounds of grass and drifted into sleep.

But Marumuruti was awake and pondering. She took the little bat, Impimpi, from her earlobe and he clung to her finger while she whispered to him. Then she tossed him into the air and Impimpi circled the cave and disappeared down a low passageway. Next, Marumuruti called to Kovankuni, who swooped with silent pinions to her shoulder. After they had spoken, Kovankuni flew off into the forest. She dallied a little among the foothills, and let it be known that she was hunting along the river banks. But when the moon had passed over and the world lay in the deep shadow of night she disappeared into the forest of the upper ridges, heading up to where the crags of Atum Oldok rose under the stars.

Later, when a ragged little shadow fluttered out of the darkness and circled her head, Marumuruti started up and held out her finger and Impimpi clung to it and settled his dusty wings. Marumuruti listened with her head on one side to a list of complaints about the route that Impimpi had had to take, how he had been floored and had floundered and crawled along winding passages where no self-respecting

45

bat should have to venture. But when he told her of what he had seen in the cave of Nalankeng, her eyes brightened. She went over and shook Tajewo by the shoulder. 'My son,' she said, 'Impimpi brings news from the cave of Nalankeng. News of an engang of people, young and old, sheep and cattle.'

'Our people?'

Marumuruti nodded. 'They can be no other.'

'Are they well?' Tajewo sat up.

'They are in darkness and afraid, but Moloch's servants throw in enough fodder to keep the beasts alive and bearing milk. Moloch watches them sometimes, like a man counting his cattle. Impimpi tells of a tall woman with a necklace of blue and white who carries a small boy on her hip.'

'Loiyan!' said Tajewo.

Marumuruti nodded. 'Tell me, is she one of those women who gasp and scream when the unexpected happens, or does she keep calm when startled? Can she keep a secret?'

Tajewo smiled. 'Loiyan is no shrieker; she is strong and to be trusted.'

'That is good,' said the old woman. 'For Moloch's eyes are on her, if I'm not mistaken, and we must be very wary. I shall send Impimpi to Loiyan your wife and find a way to tell her that they are not forgotten. Now, sleep again, Tajewo, for you have need of it.'

Marumuruti went over to the mouth of her cave and plucked a bunch of green leaves from an overhanging tree. She held them over the hearth fire until a thick yellow smoke plumed out and then she thrust them into a crevice in the wall. Soon the drowsy hum of a bee swarm grew louder and black bees crawled out over her arms. She reached in and broke off several large pieces of honeycomb;

she wrapped them in fresh leaves and stowed them in a slim grass basket.

Then she stirred her cauldron once again and sat down to watch the stars. The shadows from the firelight flickered over the walls of the cavern and the mist from the cauldron rose and fell to the rhythm of Marumuruti's quiet breathing. Pondering deeply, the old one waited for the coming of the winged shadow of Kovankuni.

4 Moloch's captives

When Kovankuni returned at last, Marumuruti had fallen asleep, her old head sunk on her chest. The owl hopped to the floor and sidled over to peck gently at her foot and the old one's eyes flew open. She gave a cavernous yawn. 'Ah, it is you, my old shadow. Tell me – what have you seen, what have you heard?'

'Moloch's messengers are busy,' Kovankuni murmured. 'Mzinzi has spread the news of Moloch's captives and crocodiles from upstream are making their way to the pools under Lolgoron.'

'And what of the Asi of Galuma?' asked Marumuruti. 'What did Kinya say to the coming of the men of Narokem?'

'I found Mother Kinya weeping, Old One. A fire burned late in her hut as she tended Father Konyok. She spoke of battles on the heaths of Galuma, of a monster swooping to the kill, of a son dead and the old father grievously wounded.'

'Ah, my Kovankuni,' Marumuruti nodded grimly, 'this is bad news indeed. In the strange way that Fate arranges, certain people need each other sorely at this time. Now we must bring them together to end a long tale.'

She rose stiffly, walked to the mouth of the cave and peered out at the stars. 'There is no time to lose. Tajewo and Meromo must leave for the high ridges. The river banks are full of spies, you say? Well then, we shall give them something to talk about … now, where did I put that honey?'

She hurried over and, leaving Kidoni and Naikosiai

asleep, she shook Tajewo and Meromo awake. As they fastened their cloaks and took up their spears, Marumuruti gave Tajewo the basket of fresh honeycombs. 'Kovankuni will guide you now up to the Ridges of Galuma, to the Old People of the Mountain, the Asi. They do not welcome strangers and are quick to draw their bowstrings. Tread softly and speak gently. Greet them first with honey. You will find a welcome for they will expect you and have great need of you. I shall send your brothers out on another errand. It is better for only two to travel to the heights, for two go unseen where four would be noticed. Go swiftly now, and do not be anxious over those in the cave of Nalankeng. I will not forsake them.'

The Mother of Mists turned to her cauldron and stirred up a mist that wrapped round Tajewo and Meromo to hide them from the prying eyes of river bank and forest. Then she ushered them out into the night to follow the shadow of Kovankuni up through the forest to the Ridges of Galuma.

Moipu trotted ahead. They listened to the patter of his feet and the pale brush of his tail was as good as a torch to them. The dog was unafraid in a world that plainsmen dread, reared as they are to fear the forest. They mistook the hooting of the patient Kovankuni for the voices of evil spirits and every time a twig snapped they remembered the cruel whips of Kumcharaza Kiboko on Lengai. Moipu knew the sounds of the forest for what they were – the trampling of browsing duiker and the rustle of a forest rat among dry leaves. He led them along a safe path through the darkness until the grey dawn seeped into the eastern sky.

They could see the path in front of them and Moipu's tail flickering ahead through tall ferns and cloaks of thick creepers. They were walking south-east along a ridge when

49

suddenly the trees thinned and they found themselves looking up at the great heads of the Galuma, rising tall against the sky. Beyond and above them all the Morning Star hung, fading slowly in the light of dawn. They stood for a moment, glad to rest, and then set their feet on the narrow path that led under the mist-shrouded cedars.

'Woh!' Suddenly Meromo, who was in the lead, staggered backwards and bumped into Tajewo. 'Woh! Look!'

'It's the end of the world!' was all Tajewo could say.

At their feet the grey rock plunged into an abyss of swirling mist. They scrambled back to the shelter of the trees and then very cautiously they moved forward and peered ahead. The path lay along a narrow ridge, like the spine of an ox. On either side the cliffs fell away into unseen depths. The abyss filled them with terror and they crouched there, unable to move from fear of falling. Kovankuni called from out of the mist above but the men clung to a boulder.

'If I move from here, I shall fall forever like a tick from the back of an ox!' quavered Meromo. Kovankuni called again, a little closer, but still the two men clung like monkeys in their mothers' fur. Then the patient Moipu trotted back to them, and Kovankuni flew down out of the mist and led them with gentle hootings, step by step up the terrible path. They learned to keep their eyes fixed only on the path at their feet until, at last, they saw ahead a huge fig tree that brooded over an outcrop of rock. Its roots grappled the boulders like the talons of an eagle and its foliage cast a deep, black shadow.

Kovankuni glided in under the canopy but Moipu stopped and stood staring at something with the hair on his neck a little raised. Meromo and Tajewo entered cautiously and peered into the darkness. The first thing they saw were three glinting arrowheads pointed at their hearts. The bowmen were small, very dark men with deep-set eyes under heavy brows. Behind them stood a fourth man. He was taller and held a spear and he was staring at Tajewo and Meromo with a hungry curiosity. Tajewo held out the bag of honeycombs and, because he had no other words, he gave them the ancient greeting of the Maasai – 'Peace be with you!'

To his surprise the young man answered, 'And peace to the travellers from far!' and he took the honey with a small, courteous bow.

'Am I dreaming or did I hear the language of the plains on the tongue of this man of the high mountain?' murmured Meromo.

'You are not mistaken,' said the young man. 'I am Kobel, son of Konyok, clan father of Galuma. I welcome you. Marumuruti sent us word of your coming.'

'How has a man of the Galuma learned to speak the language of the plains?' Meromo asked.

With a shy gesture Kobel reached out and touched his hand. 'I am seeing one half of myself for the first time,' he said. 'I, Kobel, Konyok's son, am only half a man of the Asi. My mother came from the plains long ago.'

Now the three little men, whose bows and arrows had only just been lowered and whose suspicious glances had given way to curiosity, began to speak hurriedly, pointing at the sun. 'Come,' said Kobel, 'we must go quickly. Follow me and don't be afraid of my companions.' He turned and stooped to enter a dark passage between two leaning rocks. Tajewo and Meromo followed, coughing in the musty stink of bat droppings while the three small men trod quietly at their heels.

'Even Kumcharaza's hole had a bit of light in it!' grumbled Meromo, banging his head for the third time against the rough rock ceiling and bumping into Tajewo from behind. They ignored the small sounds of stifled laughter behind them and fumbled slowly forwards to where Kobel waited, calling encouragement.

As their grumbling voices died away, Kovankuni blinked once or twice at the early morning sunlight and sidled along a branch till she was a mere shadow against the mottled trunk of the fig tree. Then she closed her golden eyes and slept.

That same morning, when the sun was high, two men were seen blundering through the shallows of Lolmoloch River. They grumbled loudly about the unfairness of a mysterious quest and seemed to be searching the caves and gullies of the kranses for something. All day long they made a show of querulous stupidity and were noted by eyes and ears in the reed beds and river banks. When dusk fell they kindled a fire on the western bank of the Lolmoloch and roasted catfish on it, talking loudly of moving off down river to search further. Indeed, next day, for those who cared to look, their footprints showed in the river sand for some distance. They followed the winding Lolmoloch as it flowed north west into the plains. Then, under the cover of night, they took a swift path into the west, travelling towards the hills of Kasithi.

Kidoni and Naikosiai ran with a message for Sirigashi. Marumuruti had rightly surmised that the old eagle would have summoned warriors from the clans of the Red Cow, ready to fight for their people, if need be. But the Mother of

Mists wished to warn Sirigashi that there must be no sign of war bands gathering unless she sent word, and that any evidence of warriors scouting near the Lolmoloch might bring ruin upon them all.

The next day at dusk Naikosiai and Kidoni loped wearily into Sirigashi's engang. When they had washed and rested, they sat beside the seer's hearth fire and the story that they told kept their listeners awake into the small hours of the morning.

A ray of sunlight shone through a crack in the roof of Nalankeng cave. It fell on the face of Loiyan, sleeping with her child in her arms and presently she stirred, feeling the warmth on her cheek. She opened her eyes and smiled, thinking at first that she was lying in her hut and had over-slept and that the sun was peering down her smoke hole, chiding her. Then her eyes wandered to the rocky walls of the cavern and she remembered. She sat up and found Nandi asleep nearby with her baby in her arms while her little Labot lay further off against the flank of Meromo's gentle red bull, his small hand clasping its neck folds protectively.

Loiyan laid her head back against a boulder and sighed. Their capture was a mystery that lay upon her like a dark cloud. Who had snatched them from their homes in the ter-rible wind? Who held them captive in this dark place? Whose was the brooding presence in the darkness? And had-n't she sensed that malign haunting before ... somewhere?

It was strange, she thought, that the enemy who held them had ordered his henchmen to throw in grass each day for the sheep and cattle, and dry dung and wood enough for a small hearth fire. The herds had soon grown accustomed to the great cavern. They lay calmly chewing cud and let down their milk at the usual times. She and Nandi and the other young women drew fresh milk each day and, being Maasai of the Narokem, they lived as they always did, proudly and with dignity from the milk and blood of their cattle. The children tended the sheep and ran errands for the old folk who still lay feeble and shaken, for to be the plaything of a whirlwind is very hard on aged joints.

Loiyan had cared tenderly for Tajewo's old parents, venturing down to the stream in the dark reaches of the cave to fetch water for them. For the first few days Tajewo's mother, old Meria, had lain groaning and lamenting and too bruised to be of use to anyone. But then, fumbling among the folds of her cloak she discovered a pouch containing her clay pipe, unbroken, and a goodly supply of tobacco. Meria's vigour returned and presently the pipe was lit and was passing from hand to hand. Somehow, reserves of courage and humour that had seemed mislaid were drawn forth and the rising smoke brought to mind the old figures of legend and fireside tale. Meria beckoned the children to her and she had not said the words 'Way back, in the old times, when men and animals still spoke to each other' more than twice before they had all crouched to listen. Parents drifted over to keep an eye on their children and soon the entire engang had gathered to hear the old stories. The blue smoke drifted slowly upwards in the shaft of sunlight and for a few hours their plight was forgotten.

When night fell and the only light in the cavern was the flickering of the small fire, Nandi and Loiyan sat huddled together, feeding the precious flames. Nandi looked round into the darkness and whispered, 'Loiyan, don't you feel as if someone is watching us? You know – the way a jackal noses a clutch of ostrich eggs.'

'Yes,' Loiyan answered. 'I feel it too. As if one is a goat in a pen – a goat about to be sacrificed,' she shivered. 'Surely our men must know that we are gone. Why has there been no sign of them?'

'But who is it they have to fight? Who has taken us and why?' Nandi sighed and presently her head fell against Loiyan's shoulder and she slept.

Loiyan could not sleep. Koki stirred in her arms and whimpered in a bad dream and she rocked him and crooned an old lullaby. When his head fell at last into the crook of her arm, Loiyan still sat staring into the darkness, wakeful and afraid. Mindful of the fading fire, she rose later to add a little fuel and as she turned away she saw a swift shadow flit across the sleeping cattle. Presently it came again – a bat fluttering to and fro and all the time circling closer to where she sat. At last it flew up and clung to the roof above her, and at the same moment something dropped into her lap. It was a dry pod tied with a wisp of grass. Loiyan's heart gave a queer little skip. In the shadow of her skirt she slid off the little grass noose and the pod halves fell open. The dry white inner skin of each seemed to be covered in tiny pictures drawn with the tip of a charcoal twig.

In the firelight she could just make out a cow and some people in a cave. 'That's us,' she thought. 'Here are four men with spears, running, and here – this is strange – is a woman with a big pot with steam rising from it. And here is a bat! That's all. It looks as if the woman is touching the bat. Or pointing to it.' She glanced up and saw that the bat was still hanging above her, watching her with tiny, twinkling eyes. 'The bat and the woman,' Loiyan mused, 'they seem to belong together. That means she is the one who has sent me this message. But why is there an empty place here, when she could have told me more?' Still the bat clung. Then it swooped and circled her head several times and then hung again. Suddenly Loiyan understood. 'I'm half asleep!' she muttered. She leaned over the fire and removed a charred grass stem. She thought carefully and then she drew a woman standing. She had a spear in one hand, 'To tell her that I'm ready to fight,' she murmured, 'and I'm holding out my other hand to show that I'm ready to take whatever she can give me. There.' She slid the grass noose round the pod halves and held the pod up in her fingers. The bat swooped from the roof, his fine claws grasped the pod and he vanished into the darkness.

Suddenly Loiyan felt less lonely. 'Somebody knows we are here,' she murmured. 'Somebody knows that four men with spears are busy, and somebody cares about us enough to let us know. I wonder who she is, this woman with the pot ...' She began to feel a stirring of hope. She drew her cloak over herself and her son and for the first time since their capture, she slept.

5 The Asi of the High Forest

As they staggered after Kobel along the secret passageway
to the heights of Galuma, Tajewo and Meromo were forced
to crouch and finally crawl. Their feet got tangled in their
cloaks, their long spears got wedged in rocky corners and
dust and bat droppings made them cough until their eyes
watered.

'If it were not for these Asi with their arrows pointed at
my hindquarters,' muttered Meromo, 'I would back out of
here like a dog out of a porcupine's lair. I feel my dignity as
an elder is being compromised.'

Just as they were beginning to feel they would die from
lack of air, Tajewo noticed that he could just see his hand
held out in front of him. Then a dim grey light illumined
the rock walls. Somewhere ahead Kobel suddenly forced his
way through a tangle of leaves and the light of day shone
through. Thankfully Tajewo crawled out and found himself in the green and golden light of a forest glade. Meromo
stumbled out and sank into the deep grass and was followed by the three little men in whose sombre eyes a twin-
kle of amusement lurked as they looked at the two plainsmen. When he had caught his breath, Meromo laughed,
pointing at Tajewo, who, like himself, was grey with dust
while bat droppings clung to his cloak and cobwebs matted
his hair. Kobel laughed too and even the little bowmen
bashfully wiped the dust from their faces.

'Come,' said Kobel, 'we must visit the Stream of the
Home Path before we go any further.'

He led them to where a stream fell into a rock pool, its

water clearer and colder than any they had known. It took their breath away as they plunged in but when they climbed out they found that the aching tiredness of the night's climb had been washed away and they were refreshed.

They followed Kobel up a twisting path to a tall iron-wood tree where he stopped and tapped the trunk and suddenly the head and shoulders of a man peered down through the foliage. He stared intently at the tall plainsmen and then disappeared. There was a rustle of leaves and then an eerie call floated above them. It was echoed by another call up ahead and then by another still further up. 'They will be ready for us,' said Kobel and strode on beneath trees hung with grey moss like the beards of ancient men.

They were indeed ready, for when Kobel led them into a clearing between great yellowwood trees, every man, woman and child in his village had gathered. The shy Asi folk of the high ridges stood in a silent half circle, staring at the giants from the plains. The men were stony faced, their features betraying no emotion, but their deep-set eyes were wary. Several women put their hands to their mouths to hide their alarm and small children scattered, screaming, only to reappear, clutching their fathers' legs, to stare at the strange tall, thin men from far away. Kobel spoke the Asi tongue as they came into the village and a murmur of deep voices rose as the people moved back and let them pass. He led them across the clearing to a group of three huts at the far side. 'Come,' he said quietly, 'the old ones are waiting.'

They stooped to enter the central hut. Kobel went and knelt down beside a bed of colobus skins where an old man was lying. He opened his eyes at Kobel's greeting and with great effort laid his hand on Kobel's arm and whispered a few words.

'Father Konyok welcomes you,' said Kobel. 'He is grieved

that he cannot rise to greet you, but since he was wounded by the talons of Geraragua a fever has laid hold of him that none of our medicines can cure.'

Tajewo and Meromo came forward to greet Father Konyok and as his old eyes flickered open they found themselves looking at a face full of strength and authority.

Now Kobel turned to another old man with a deep brow and snowy hair who sat watching them out of keen eyes. 'This is Father's brother, Gurum,' he said. 'For the time being he is Father of the Ridge in Father Konyok's place.' Gurum greeted them first in his own tongue and then in halting phrases of Maasai and the eager old hands that grasped theirs were full of power and warmth. Tajewo and Meromo gazed with respect at this man who stood far below their shoulders, yet was as full of sinewy power as a man in his prime on the plains.

Then, from behind a hide curtain, an old woman emerged. She stood looking at them with the same hungry wonder they had seen in Kobel's face. She had the slim, hawk's face of those who had come long ago from the north. For a moment she stared, her eyes travelling from their heads to their feet, then she came closer and they saw tears gathering in her eyes. 'Sons of the Narokem,' she said huskily, 'I have not set eyes on my kin since I was a child. You are welcome guests in my place. You have news for me, I know, but you have come a long way and are weary. We shall talk when you are rested. Know yourselves welcome and honoured.'

Tajewo and Meromo were glad to stumble across to Kobel's hut and sink into piles of grey bedding bush, covered with hyrax skins, and fall asleep. It was dusk when Kobel woke them and led them out to sit with his people round the big fire where roasted meat was brought to them and honey beer was passed between them and the men of the clan as a sign of friendship.

But when an owl hooted in the darkness beyond the fire-light Kobel took them away to Konyok's hut, and there in the golden light of her hearth fire sat Kinya, laying crushed leaves on Konyok's wound. Perched on a roof branch was Kovankuni the wood owl. When Kinya had drawn a soft hide over the sleeping Konyok she turned to them and suddenly smiled through her weariness. 'I still cannot believe that I see my own kinsmen, as if time had fallen away, as if I were a child again. For I was born on the plains near the hills of Narok, of the Black Cow clan. When I was still a young child there was a time of famine, followed by the sickness that ate up our cattle. I remember how we went searching, in the heat of the day, for roots and leaves to eat. I remember the sharp pain of hunger that made a child chew on an old hide sandal or the bark of a thorn tree. When we lay down at night no one knew who would rise from their sleeping mat at dawn, or who would not...' Kinya stared into the hearth embers. 'The hyenas grew as bold as the dogs of the engang. How often I saw their eyes in the darkness beyond the doorway.

'One day, of all my family, it was only I who rose at dawn. I walked alone to the Kutum River which was only sand among stones, to dig up little bitter bulbs in the river bank. I came to the small forest near the river and I sat down and cried because I was small and alone. Out of the bushes a boy came, a boy who was almost a man, with a bow and arrow and two birds hanging in his hand. I spoke to him in my tongue and he answered in his tongue and we could not understand each other. Yet his eyes under those thick brows were very kind.' Kinya glanced over at the sleeping Konyok. 'Yes, it was Konyok. He held out his hand to me and took me into the forest, to his people, and I have belonged here with them ever since.

'And all has been well with us,' Kinya said, 'for we live far from warring tribes and famine does not touch the people of the Galuma, for the spirit of the forest watches over his children. But now something has happened that has never happened before. At the coming of the last rains, as the thunderheads began to build over the heights of the Shira, a creature came out of the caverns of Atum Oldok.

'Geraragua, we call it, after the crags like rotten teeth where it lives. It is a lizard-headed, bat-winged creature, cruel and monstrous, with curved talons full of filth. Like a vulture it swoops down on the kills that others make. A buffalo bull is a single meal and a grazing eland or a man is a mere morsel. Look –' she drew back the covering and they saw on Konyok's breast a jagged, suppurating wound in his swollen flesh. 'That is what the claws of Geraragua do to a man.' Gently she covered him again and tears of despair filled her eyes.

'Ten days ago we brought down a buffalo on the heath of Teldeg, just above the forest here,' said Kobel. 'Father Konyok's arrow had penetrated below the ear and to him fell the honour of the death thrust. As he stood beside the beast to raise his spear, Geraragua fell upon us out of the sky. He raked Father Konyok with his talons, as a hawk does a mouse, and grappled the buffalo and rose with it into the sky.'

'We carried my father home, stopping first to wash his wounds in the stream of the Teldeg,' Kobel said. 'But something of Geraragua's evil filth is in his flesh. He is failing.'

'I've culled all the herbs of the mountain and pounded bark and root for him,' said Kinya. 'I've made compresses and potions, but nothing has drawn the poison from

Konyok's breast. I am afraid his heart cannot beat against it much longer.' Her slim wrinkled hand reached over and gently touched the old man's forehead.

'Since Geraragua began to haunt the mountain, our lives have become like those of the small creatures who cannot leave their burrows without fearing the hawk. His evil eyes pick out everything that moves between the forest's edge and the heights of Shira, even a woman venturing into the heath lands to cull herbs, or a child hunting the little partridges that run below the grass.'

'What is Geraragua like?' asked Meromo.

'He is most like a lizard but between his front legs and his sides the skin has stretched into wings,' said Kobel. 'His curved talons are as long and sharp as my spearhead. He is bigger than ten bull elephants, yet he can circle as swiftly as a vulture and fall on us out of the sky like a stone. There is only one place that he fears and it is the forest, for once he is among the trees he cannot fly.'

Tajewo and Meromo looked at one another. 'This is indeed the creature that Marumuruti told us of – a lizard of the rocks grown monstrous. Somewhere inside his body the Stone of Naiterogop must be lodged.'

'And we shall only find it by killing the creature,' said Meromo. 'It seems we have a terrible task to perform, brother.'

Kobel was watching them eagerly. 'To slay Geraragua is our hearts' desire,' he said. 'Almost every night when the fire falls to embers the men of the Galuma sit and talk of hunting him. We have tried to defend our prey, but the buffalo and eland that we hunt on the grasslands are taken from us and those who have tried to fight Geraragua have become his prey as well.' Kobel shuddered and his head fell on his breast. 'My brother, Kibwere, was killed when he stood up bravely to defend the body of an eland bull he'd killed. As Geraragua flew down over him he thrust his spear into Geraragua's belly. But…my brother became his prey.' Kobel was silent while Gurum and Mother Kinya brushed tears from their cheeks and Tajewo sensed a grief too raw to be spoken of. Kobel's eyes smouldered with anger: 'There are many families among us now who wish to see Geraragua dead. Yet we cannot see a way. For we must lure him into the forest if we are to stand a chance.'

'Is there any place on his body that a spear might pierce, if it is driven with great force?' asked Tajewo.

'We have seen him from close by now several times,' Kobel answered. 'But it seems that there is nowhere except through the eyes and perhaps the throat where a spear could enter deep enough to kill him. But only a man with long arms and a long spear would be able to give Geraragua the death thrust – and we Asi of the Galuma are small men, as you see. Even I am only half plainsman!' he added ruefully.

Mother Kinya had listened in silence while they spoke and now she raised her eyes and looked long and thoughtfully at Tajewo and Meromo. 'I do not know yet why the old Mother of Mists has sent you to us. I see that you are not altogether surprised to hear of Geraragua. The old night bird who flies between Marumuruti and myself has told me that you have troubles of your own. It seems to me that now two troubled paths have run together. Will you not tell us the story of your journey and your quest?'

Kinya laid a branch of fragrant olive wood over the fire. Then the hut was silent while she, Kobel and Gurum listened to the story of the journey to Lengai, of Moloch's revenge for Ndamathia's humiliation and, last of all, the tale of how the tear of the Morning Star had passed from

the hands of Naiterogop, down through countless generations, and had come to rest in the body of Geraragua.
When at last the tale was told the fire had fallen into ash but
the eyes of Kinya and Kobel had kindled with wonder and
hope.

'It will be honey on my tongue if my own kinsmen of the
long straight spears could repay my debt to Konyok who
granted me life long ago,' said Kinya, looking at the old man
lying shivering in pain. 'You will find that every man and
woman and child among us will help with the hunting of
Geraragua.'

'Old Mother,' Tajewo answered, 'it is as you have said;
our paths have indeed run together and our purposes are
now one purpose. You wish for the dead body of Geraragua
and we seek the stone that lies within it. Our spear arms
and our warrior skills are yours.'

'How many men here will hunt with us?' asked Meromo.

'There are twenty in our clearing who still hunt the
buffalo,' said Kobel. 'But that is nothing against Geraragua.
I shall send out the call tomorrow at dawn and we shall
have twice fifty by twilight. Then we can talk of hunting.'

'Men of the Narokem,' Kinya said, 'Kobel must leave you
to rest now, though I can see from his face that he would
like to spend the last hours of the night talking. But if you
are to rise at dawn then you must rest. Peace be upon your
sleeping.'

Hearing the peace blessing in their own tongue, they felt
suddenly at home in the strange forest realm. They rose
and went to sleep in Kobel's hut. But Kobel sat outside,
staring up at the stars, bitter and vengeful, full of longing
and self-doubt and half-formed plans.

Presently he went over to the big fire where Gurum sat
staring pensively into the glowing embers. 'You too?' said

the old man quietly. 'The torment of remembering and the desire to avenge a father and a brother keep sleep away. So, it is better to stay awake and plan, brother's son. Let us begin to gather our wits for a great battle.'

6   The Calling

Tajewo and Meromo were woken at dawn by Kobel who whispered, 'Come and watch the Calling!'

'What Calling?' mumbled Meromo, still only half aware of where he was.

'We'll be calling the hunters of Galuma,' Kobel answered.

'Hmph,' Meromo rolled over to sleep again when suddenly he remembered. 'The hunters? The hundred men for the hunting of Geraragua?'

'The same,' said Kobel. 'We must hurry, for Kapasiso is impatient.'

They rose and wrapped their cloaks round them and followed Kobel to where a powerful little man with jutting brows waited silently beside the village fire. He nodded at their greeting and turned and led them into the forest mist. They walked swiftly up the eastern ridge till they came to an ironwood tree from which thick grey lianas hung. Kapasiso grasped one and shinned upwards with the ease of a grey monkey. Kobel followed him and then peered down at them. 'Come up, brothers. There is nothing to fear.'

The plainsmen looked at each other uneasily. It was years since they had swung from forest trees as boys and they stared with misgiving into the misty foliage above. Kobel shook a branch challengingly. 'Surely my honourable kinsmen are not afraid?' he taunted. 'They are merely a little out of practice – like some of the eldest elders of my clan?'

Meromo snorted and grasped a long grey creeper. Painfully, with grunts of effort, he hauled himself up onto a branch beside Kobel. Then he peered down at Tajewo. 'Let these tree apes not look down for long upon an elder of the Narokem!' he said and he watched with a certain painful satisfaction as Tajewo grappled and swung on the grey rope.

By now Kapasiso was a mere rustle in the leaves far above and Kobel's legs were disappearing overhead. They climbed up beside him and when they looked down they froze and clung to the trunk for the whole world had fallen away at their feet. Far below, the forested spurs of the mountain sank into misted valleys and east, above the forest, rose the bare mountain heath. Beyond and above all, in the light of the rising sun, shone the wings of Kibo.

Then, high overhead, a call went floating like a bird: 'Oh-oooooh-oh! Oh-ooooooh!' Winging away to the south and to the west. 'Oh-ooooooooooh-oh!' Sending his voice out like a hawk on the wind across the great valleys, Kapasiso called to the clans of the high forest. At last a distant call came back. Kapasiso called again and was answered by calls from the south and west. Then the little man came shinning down from the crown of the tree, to where Tajewo and Meromo still clung to their perch. 'It is done,' he said. 'They will be with us before sunset.'

Lithely he and Kobel swung to the ground while Tajewo and Meromo slithered painfully after them. Kobel was laughing. 'Well, was it not a thing worth seeing, kinsmen?'

'If you are one of those who enjoy dangling like a rat in a hawk's talons,' muttered Tajewo, picking moss and dry twigs from his cloak.

'It put me in mind of a misadventure we had many years ago,' said Meromo, remembering with a shudder how they had dealt with the eagle Tangwembe on Mount Lengai. 'I would have been content to admire the Calling from a humble position among the roots,' he laughed ruefully. 'However, I will never forget it. Now, take us back to that safe place on the firm ground where there is a fire and maybe something to fill a man's stomach.'

Chuckling, Kapasiso and Kobel led them at a swift trot back to the village. Presently they met a posse of boys carrying long green leaves and a basket of embers. 'Ha – the little honey gatherers,' said Kobel. In the Asi tongue he added, 'Talk kindly to our bees for it is their sweetness that will give us strength for our hunting!' The children ducked past them respectfully and ran on to visit the log hives that are the most treasured possessions of the mountain people.

The village glade was quiet when they came there. Old Gurum was standing before a group of men equipped for a buffalo hunt. The rest of the village looked on in silence while Gurum chanted a prayer for luck in hunting and then sprayed honey beer over the hunters.

'It is the prayer that they may be guided to find a herd of buffalo, for without buffalo we cannot summon Geraragua. Everything depends on their success,' said Kobel.

Gurum's chanting rose to a shout, then it ceased and in silence the hunters turned and filed away into the forest. The eyes of the villagers followed them and Tajewo saw how their hearts and hopes went with the scouts.

Then the village swarmed to life like a beehive. Women went into their huts and came out dragging hunting nets. They brought them to the space near the fire and fetched thongs and sinews with which to sew them together into one big net. And the old men came over to relieve their feelings of envy and anxiety by pointing out the weak places in the netting with loud criticism. Younger men who had been whittling at long, sharp staves took them up in loads over their shoulders and disappeared along a path leading away south.

'Where are they going?' Tajewo asked.

'To the pit in the Nairob ravine,' said Kobel. 'Whilst you were sleeping Gurum called the elders and warriors and we sat in council together. The hunting of Geraragua is a very great undertaking and many things have to come together.

'All those who sat and debated are agreed. There is only one place where we can trap and kill Geraragua. It is where the Nairob stream flows down from Ol Gelene hill into the forest. Where the stream enters the forest there is an open space between tall trees. Here we can dig a great pit of stakes. We shall drive a herd of buffalo over Ol Gelene hill into the ravine and then head them downhill. From his perch on Atum Oldok Geraragua will see the buffalo running and, as he has done before, he will make use of it. He will soar up and then fall upon a beast as they run down into the ravine. We must prevent him from flying up with his kill and returning safely to Atum Oldok. Instead we shall lure him further and further down, to try again and again, until he goes too far and flounders into the place where the Nairob flows into the forest, headlong into the pit of staves. From the trees nearby we shall cast our hunting nets to snare his wings – and his tail which can destroy a man with a sideways blow.'

It was just then that Meromo's stomach made such loud protesting sounds that Kobel interrupted himself and apologised. 'I have neglected our guests in all this hurry,' he muttered. 'Forgive me.' He darted off to return with skewers of meat that had lain forgotten on the hearth-stones.

When they had eaten, Tajewo, who had been pondering the strategy of the hunt with a thoughtful frown, said, 'You have told us how you hope to trap Geraragua, my son, but when we have him, how will the death blow be dealt?'

'Twice in my lifetime – only twice it has been,' Kobel said, 'we have caught an elephant in a stave pit. The cries brought us running from far away. There were those who said let the beast cry and death would come slowly as the stakes in its belly did their work. But my father Konyok – he was still a strong hunter then – looked at the elephant. I think he saw not just meat but one who, like us, wishes to live. One who has young to love and who feels pain and fears death. My father lifted his spear and he fixed his eye on the eye of the elephant and he sent his spear in one long, sharp flash to the place here,' Kobel touched his neck below the ear, 'which kills quickly.' Kobel's eyes were full of wonder in his remembering – remembering how great a hunter Konyok his father had been and how he had loved and respected him. 'The elephant looked surprised and it gave a great sigh, breathing out. Its trunk fell, its eyes closed. It died. And Konyok, my father, saluted the elephant and sang its praises loudly before anyone dared to lay a knife into its flesh.'

'So. You finish the hunting with the spear thrust,' said Tajewo. 'May I hold your spear, kinsman?'

Kobel held out his spear. Tajewo took it and weighed it and examined the blade carefully and handed it to Meromo who measured it against his own. It was only half as long and very much lighter than a Maasai spear. 'How,' said Tajewo slowly, 'are we to deal Geraragua his death blow? Or will he perish on the stakes?'

'This we have not yet decided,' Kobel answered. 'If all goes well and Geraragua rushes into the pit of ironwood stakes we reckon that his great weight will impale him, that he will be grievously wounded and unable to rise. Yet, it can take an elephant seven days to die if it is left – that I know from the old men. How much longer it would take Geraragua I don't know.'

'We do not have the time to wait and see,' said Meromo. 'We have to return to Moloch at Lolgoron by the first night of new moon. We shall have to kill Geraragua as soon as we have caught him.'

Tajewo nodded. 'It is the only way. It will have to be spear thrusts that despatch him.'

Kobel's eyes went to his spear with an expression of intense longing. He reached for it, where it lay beside the spears of his Maasai kinsmen. But when he grasped it his spear seemed changed. It had lain beside the long spears of the most famous spearmen under the sun. It was light and weak and suddenly Kobel felt ashamed. He remembered how the light Asi spear had been his brother's undoing. 'Our spears are nothing against the power of Geraragua,' he said. 'We were hunting eland near Ol Gelene and Kibwere, my brother, brought down a fine bull. As he stood upon a rock and raised his spear for the death blow, Geraragua came rushing down to take his kill. Kibwere stood up, straight and proud on the rock and menaced the great one with his spear. But Geraragua opened his mouth,' Kobel put his hand over his eyes to blot out a memory too terrible to bear, 'his tongue, which is forked and black, swept out like a whip round Kibwere's body. Kibwere's spear snapped like a small twig. Geraragua opened his jaws like a chameleon that takes a fly and … Kibwere was gone.' Tajewo and Meromo watched in silent respect as Kobel brushed the tears off his cheeks. 'For that alone,' he said huskily, 'for the death of my brother Kibwere, and the wounding of Father Konyok, I owe Geraragua the sharpness of my spear. I cannot rest until I have avenged my kin.'

Then Tajewo did a thing that Kobel never afterwards for-got. He took Kobel's spear shaft in his strong hands and cracked it. He threw the two halves on the ground and stood up.

'Come!' he said. 'This boy's stick lies broken. Let us find our kinsman the spear of a man. Kobel,' he pulled the wondering youth to his feet, 'take us to the ravine of Nairob. Let us see where we will wage this battle.'

And Kobel, not sure whether he trod the earth of the path or floated upon some strange cloud, led them away into the forest.

While Kobel was conferring with Meromo and Tajewo, everyone in the village was busy preparing for the great hunt. Several old men sat in a patch of sunlight sharpening arrowheads on a stone, dipping them into a tiny pot of brown poison and then laying them carefully to dry. Women who were working over the hunting nets sent children to the stream to fetch water and Mother Kinya sat stitching a quiver of buck hide. She was sitting somewhat apart, in the deep shadow of a yellowwood, and presently she uttered a little crooning call. A wood owl, unseen in the branches above her, answered with a soft hoot and Kinya, seeming to mutter to herself alone, murmured at length to Kovankuni. Kovankuni flew on silent wings into the eaves of the forest stretching east towards Atum. Before midday two ravens sped up the wind to alight among the kranses of Atum Oldok. When the scaly head of Geraragua poked out of his lair to savour the warmth of the sun, he overheard a loud conversation amongst a gathering of ravenkind. There was talk of a buffalo hunt. Of men-scouts moving in the northern ridges, searching. No doubt, gossiped the ravens, the beasts would be driven out on the grasslands for the kill. Word had gone out that there would be rich pickings for those whose eyes were trained upon the Nairob valley. Geraragua dragged himself onto the warm rocks of Atum Oldok and looked hungrily over the mountain slopes below.

Very late, when children had retired to sleep, and when meat and honey beer had been brought by their women, the men sat on round the village fire and though some nodded and others leaned to sleep against companionable shoulders, everyone was waiting. All eyes lingered hopefully on the paths that entered the glade from north, south and west. At last, silently, they came, the little bands of clansmen, in answer to the Calling. One after another, speechless from the long day's walking, heavily burdened with nets and stakes, they sank down and accepted the food and drink held out by the old men.

They had little need of words. Joyfully old names were called, and greetings were simple and heartfelt. For all were kin and there was not a clan of the high forest that had not lost a son or father to the talons of Geraragua. Throughout the night they came, slipping in to eat and drink and sleep away their weariness in the light of the village fire.

But Tajewo and Meromo lifted Kobel, who had fallen asleep between them, and led him to his hut. For that day Kobel had felt what it is to handle and throw the long, swift spear of the Narokem. He had had to learn in hours what his kinsmen had learned in moons and every sinew in his body ached and his bones had turned to milk. And the spear that he still held clenched in his right hand was the long, deadly, two-ended weapon of the Maasai warrior.

At dawn the clansmen shouldered their hunting gear and melted into the forest while Tajewo and Meromo followed Kobel to the ravine of Nairob. All day they ran and hurled their spears at a target the size of a shield in the red earth of the ravine. They showed Kobel how to shift his hand along the shaft to control the balance, how to throw and how to thrust, how the leaf blade differs from the pointed stabbing end and how to draw the strength of his whole body together into his spear arm for a death thrust. At last they leaned back to rest, their chests heaving, and Meromo laid his hand on Kobel's shoulder and said, 'The blood of the Narokem ancestors is here, brother. This monkey of the high forest is becoming a lion of the plains.'

At dusk they looked down on the valley of Nairob and paused suddenly. Where a hundred men had swarmed at work, the valley was deserted. There was no sign of the pit of stakes, only the soft green grass of the valley that stretched unbroken between the banks of the forest. A lonely nightjar trilled where men and boys had toiled only an hour ago.

In the village clearing the smoke of the evening fire was rising, and the pit diggers and net menders sat eating slowly, with glazed eyes; some had fallen asleep already with food in their hands. Kinya's daughters went quietly between them with gourds of cold spring water. Then a hush fell over the glade and the women covered sleeping men and boys with soft hide cloaks so that the night chill should not stiffen their limbs.

The embers faded in the great fire and the cold dew fell, but the old ones, Kinya and Gurum among them, sat up and waited with their eyes on the forest pathway, for the scouts had not yet returned. Late, when the waning moon sent a shaft of pale light through the branches of a yellow-wood tree, Gurum rose to his feet. A dry twig snapped under his foot and woke Tajewo, who witnessed something he never forgot – the little man of the forest communing with his Great Spirit. Gurum lifted a piece of honeycomb in his hands and his deep voice rose in a chant. Tajewo could not understand the words but he knew that it was the heart of Gurum that spoke to the heart of the Great Spirit, beseeching Him to protect his people and give them good fortune in the hunting of Geraragua. For death hung over them and fear haunted the high places. As he called to the Great Spirit, the golden tears of honey dripped from Gurum's fingers and hissed among the flames and tears coursed down his face while a groan rose from Kinya and the other watchers, a groan from deep within the heart.

Tajewo slept again but started awake at the sound of thudding feet. They saw the old watchers rise eagerly to welcome the scouts who came stumbling in to stand near the fire with their hands on their knees and their chests heaving from the long day's chase. Their hair was wild with leaves and their sweat ran in golden rivers. But they looked up at Gurum and Kinya and nodded. 'Buffalo – we found them! In the valley of Njororuet. When the sun touches the wings of Kibo, we run them out!'

7 The hunting of Geraragua

Beyond Kibo the golden flush of dawn was stealing into the sky. In silence the world of the high ridges waited. Then the clear voice of a lark rose above the mountain heath and it was echoed by the voice of a man as Gurum stood up on a web of woven hide in a saptet tree and called out the hunter's prayer to God. On all sides his chant was echoed by the supplications of the Asi hunters. For each knew in his heart there are certain things a man can do: he can trim his bow and speed his arrow with a practised arm, he can sharpen his staves to perfection and double the knots in his hunting net. But only God knows where the wind will take the arrow or whether the hunted beast will turn to right or left when the last moment is upon it.

Tajewo and Meromo perched beside Kobel in a tree that rose above the forest canopy and commanded a sweeping view of the Nairob ravine and Ol Gelene hill. They kept looking towards the teeth of Shira, the high crags beyond which the white wings of Kibo would shine out in the first rays of the rising sun. At that moment, the scouts had promised, they would begin to drive the buffalo out of the Njororuet valley onto the mountain heath.

Silence hung over the Nairob. Nothing moved except small flocks of ravens winging down from the mountain heights and gathering in large, croaking assemblies to circle the Ol Gelene. Then suddenly the golden sun shot its beams into the sky and a sighing sound flowed through the trees like wind. Men moved restlessly among the branches, craning to peer north towards the Njororuet.

It was Meromo who first murmured, 'Thunder – very faint, in the north.'

'Not thunder,' answered Kobel, 'buffalo running.'

They gazed over the brown heath sweeping up to the rounded hill of Ol Gelene and suddenly they saw it – a dark mass in the distance, seething out of the forest and up the hillside. 'Here they come,' Kobel muttered. 'Drive them well, and keep them coming south. Not too fast, or they will scatter the beaters!'

'But where are the beaters?' asked Tajewo.

'You see those white dots up there among the heath bushes? Those are beaters' shields, daubed with white clay. As the buffalo herd approaches, they'll rise and beat their shields with gourds. The din will scare the buffalo into running south and stop them dispersing up the mountain slopes. This way they drive them along the route we want them to take – over the hill of Ol Gelene where Geraragua will see them. From the heights of Atum Oldok, up there, he'll make his forays. He'll soar up and then swoop down over the running herd. Several times we must let him think he is about to make a kill, but we must not let him take his beast until the herd is running right into the forest. It is only here we can do battle with him.'

Shading their eyes against the morning sun, Tajewo and Meromo stared until they made out the line of white shields in the distance.

'But how can they possibly turn a herd of buffalo?' Meromo was incredulous. 'Surely those tiny dots will be crushed and trampled as the beasts thunder out on the mountain?'

'It is all in the timing,' said Kobel. 'If they leave their warning too late they will be trampled to death. There is nothing like that thought to get a man jumping up and shouting and banging in good time.' He smiled. 'I've done it myself and I can tell you that long before you leap up to bang your shield your heart is beating loudly enough to frighten a hundred buffalo! Aha!' he pointed at another flock of ravens that came flying slowly along the forest's edge, 'our wind-folk are gathering.'

From a nearby tree came a sudden cry. Kobel swung round and peered south east. 'Look,' he said, ' look up at the cliffs!'

Where Atum Oldok rose against the sky a dark shape was moving. For a moment it hunched upon a towering buttress of rock and then it launched itself into the air – a monstrous lizard with wings. A sighing hiss of alarm came from the Asi. 'Now the battle is beginning,' Kobel gripped a branch till his knuckles shone and watched the buffalo thundering up to the slopes of Ol Gelene. 'Beseech the Great Spirit that Geraragua does not swoop too soon. If he panics the buffalo now they will charge back into the forest and trample our beaters. Then we have lost the fight. No – you old murderer! Not yet, not yet!'

Geraragua came circling slowly westwards and then he spiralled up into the sky, growing smaller and smaller as if about to vanish altogether. 'You don't deceive us, you vile lizard,' growled Kobel. 'You soar beyond our sight and then drop like a stone upon us. Oh hurry! Hurry those beasts along! Get them off the Ol Gelene.' He shook the branch in his urgency. Tajewo and Meromo craned their necks to follow the gyres of the circling monster, their eyes watering in the bright sunlight.

Then a groaning sigh swept through the trees as Geraragua hurtled out of the sky. 'Too soon, too soon!' groaned Kobel. 'They're still too far from the Nairob. He'll scatter them into the forest – our men will be trampled!' But, as

Geraragua descended, a flock of ravens came speeding out of the forest, hurling themselves at his head like furious bees, clinging and pecking at his eyes.

'Yes, yes, turn him! Don't let him strike yet!' Kobel cried.

Plagued by the tormenting birds, Geraragua swerved aside and soared up to circle again.

'Drive them, men, drive them over to Ol Gelene! Ah! Have you ever seen running like that?' Kobel's eyes shone. 'Nothing on the mountain sounds better than the thunder of that running. Yes, send them over, send them down!' He looked up, shading his eyes. 'Now let the old devil try – we'll need the ravens, though...'

From high above them there came a chilling screech of fury as Geraragua plunged earthwards. The buffalo herd panicked and split. Some rushed down into the forest and others thundered over the Ol Gelene towards the shelter of Nairob ravine. And again the cloud of birds swarmed at Geraragua's head, blinding him so that he missed his prey. He rose again with a hiss of baffled fury, just as the herd rushed bellowing into the Nairob ravine.

They never forgot the charge of the buffalo down the valley. The thunder of their hooves shook the ground and a cloud of red dust billowed in their wake. An exulting shout rose from the trees. Again Geraragua swooped with desperate fury and was plagued by the raven flocks. Yet he raked the back of a cow and sent the herd bellowing in panic downhill. As he rose, the men glimpsed the long, yellow belly, the talons dripping blood, the armour of black and yellow skin folds on neck and face. The huge jaws opened in a venomous hiss. 'The size of him!' said Meromo, 'Our spears are as puny as twigs compared to those jaws!'

'Engai shield us!' muttered Tajewo.

'Now!' Kobel smacked a branch with his hand. 'It must

be now! Yes, yes! He knows. It's his last chance. Slow them, slow them a little, Tamek. Yes – they must hesitate just a little, while he gains height for his last drop. Ah. Look! He's circling again. Now, watch him!'

Everything happened with terrible swiftness. Geraragua fell upon the herd as it ran down into the Nairob valley. The wind of his vast wings beat upon the treetops and men clung fiercely to branches. Kobel fixed his eyes on the spot where the Nairob ravine entered the forest. 'May the Great Spirit defend Kapasiso now!' he said. Kapasiso crouched at the head of the covered pit. As the buffaloes came down he would rise with his white shield and divide them into two streams to flow on either side of the pit. For if they ran into the pit it would be revealed to Geraragua.

'Now!' shrieked Kobel. 'Now, Kapasiso!'

And Kapasiso rose. As the black herd in the dust-cloud thundered down towards him, he stood up and beat upon his white shield. At that moment Geraragua sank his talons into the back of a great bull and the bellowing, panicking mass charged down on the little man. Kapasiso went down under the thundering hooves, but behind him, to left and right Kamek and Nandet also rose and beat upon their shields. The herd divided, swerved aside to left and right and thundered away into the safety of the forest.

Geraragua, seeing his only chance of a kill, grappled the bull in his back talons, and beat his huge wings to rise into the air. But he had gone just too far into the valley and the forest was closer than his greed had let him see. His wings snagged on the trees and he crashed headlong. Smashing forest trees, like a rockslide on a high mountain he sank over the pit and the huge weight of his underbelly dragged him down upon the stakes. With a croak of fury, he gouged the marshy soil with his claws but his thrashing was in vain.

He reared his head and uttered a venomous hiss as a hail of stinging arrows winged towards his eyes and stone-weighted nets flew into the air to entangle his thrashing wings. Men ran in to pin the great webs to the ground with stakes.

'We have him now!' cried Kobel. 'His blood is flowing. It is time to go down and fight.'

He ran into the valley followed by Tajewo and Meromo. But before they'd gone far, three men came towards them, carrying the brave little Kapasiso to the shelter of the trees, a small inert bundle wrapped in a hide cloak. Gurum and Kobel approached anxiously. 'Does his heart still beat?' Kobel reached out to touch his still shoulder.

'It beats still, but he is bleeding from the mouth, for he was trampled. I don't like it much,' said Gurum. 'Take him quickly over to Kapimot; he knows best what to do now. And hurry back – the battle is only beginning!'

Just then from the forest edge came the shrill ululations of women and children. From a point of safety they had witnessed Geraragua's trapping and now they pressed close among the trees, to watch the final battle. Though forbidden to enter the valley, they stood waiting to receive the wounded, and Mother Kinya had brought compresses of crushed leaves, roots and bark. A wailing sigh wafted from the women as Kapasiso was carried up to them, followed by Nandet and Kamek, half-stumbling, half-dragged by their companions.

Then Gurum raised his arms and gave a shout and his men moved in towards the pit. Suddenly Geraragua's tail swept round like a whip and sent men spinning into the air to fall winded a spear's throw away.

'Wait! Back, my warriors!' shouted Gurum. 'Play this game carefully! Tire the beast but do not become his meat!'

He drove off some of the younger men, too eager to use their spears. 'He is not finished yet – look! Fools – while you play with his tail he is preparing to slash you with his talons! He knows well how to fight! Take your stand at the very tip of the tail and you there – take positions just beyond the reach of the forefeet!'

Under the stern eyes of Gurum and his old warriors, the young men with their speed and strength taunted the huge lizard until the thrashing tail had been entangled in throwing nets and the huge claw-tipped wings and forefeet had been staked to the ground.

When, at last, Geraragua was pinioned, Gurum motioned his fighters back. 'He is tiring,' he said. 'We have done what we can. Now only the three spearmen can bring this to an end.'

'Stand close by, in case we need you,' said Tajewo. 'If it goes badly with us, you must distract him by attacking the tail. Now, may Engai shield us!'

'Take care – remember Kibwere!' called Gurum. 'That tongue stretches many lengths of a man!'

The three spearmen walked slowly towards Geraragua. His evil head was twice the height of a man. The eyes were almost closed between the armoured lids, but the straight hard jaws that had crushed the limbs of men and buffalo as if they were the frail bones of francolin were slightly open. As they moved forward they heard an unearthly and malevolent hissing sound.

Tajewo stared intently at Geraragua's eyes and glimpsed the movement of oily black pupils. 'He is watching us,' he said. 'He is not so tired that he cannot follow our moves.'

Then he darted forward, brandishing his spear. Geraragua's jaws gaped and out of orange depths rose the black tongue. Tajewo sprang back as it whipped towards him.

It was a tongue as long and sinewy as a python and it came towards him with the accuracy of a well-aimed arrow. Suddenly Kobel darted in from behind Tajewo and stabbed the spiked end of his spear into the tongue. 'That is for my brother, Kibwere!' he shouted. But his desire for revenge spoke louder than his warrior's skill, for the spear was wrenched from his hand as Geraragua whipped his tongue back into his mouth. The spear fell to the ground so close to the head that to retrieve it would be certain death.

In a flash Tajewo took hold of Kobel's arm, pulling him back to safety. Kobel stood disarmed, the great spear that was his pride lost before he had even engaged in his first fight, so carefully rehearsed. Too ashamed to look at his mentor, he hung his head and hot tears of anguish spurted over his cheeks. 'I have shamed you,' he said. 'I'm not worthy to fight beside you now.'

'Brother, all is not lost,' urged Tajewo. 'We will do as we have planned and we cannot do it without you. You must retrieve your spear. Watch carefully for that chance and it will come. Now I am going in! Once I am in the mouth, do not look at me. I live or die, as Engai wishes. Only do what we have agreed to do. The rest is with God. Now, be ready – my right hand and my left hand!'

Slowly he walked toward the great head. He noted the black eyes sliding to follow his steps and he sensed the cold malice of Geraragua. He raised his spear and tossed it, spinning into the air so that it dazzled like a sunbird in flight. He caught it and danced forward, feinting from side to side, darting this way and that and all the time uttering the hoarse chants of a warrior who sallies out to challenge a heavy-maned lion.

Closer he came and closer, shouting insults yet never losing sight of the cunning eyes. When Geraragua's jaws opened, like a cave opening in a head of granite, Tajewo was ready. He raised his arms high, keeping them free as the great black tongue lashed out. He felt its snake-strength wrap round his waist and pull tight, so tight that the blood rushed into his face and his eyes started from his head. He rose into the air and hung for a terrible moment while a groan went up from the men on the ground. But his arms and his spear hung free – his great, two-ended spear of blade and spike.

A fierce tug of the reptile's tongue drew him into the mouth. Then, as the great jaws closed over him, Tajewo drew the last strength of his battered body into his arms. He gripped his spear in both hands and gave it a quick twist so that the spear blade pointed straight up and the long spike pointed down. As Geraragua snapped his mouth shut, the upper jaw fell on the blade and drove the spiked end arm-deep into the flesh of the lower jaw. In agony Geraragua opened his mouth and his huge jaws gaped wide, exposing the soft orange flesh of his throat. With a shout Meromo leaped up onto the lower jaw and plunged his spear into the roots of the tongue.

Kobel, watching for his chance, ran in to retrieve his spear. At the same moment Geraragua shook his head in a spasm of fury. The horny armour of his throat caught Kobel, tearing open his back and sending him flying across the ground. A cry went up from his kin as Kobel's blood spread in a red cloak over his back. But he staggered to his feet and ran in again. This time he watched more carefully and when Geraragua slewed his head to one side Kobel darted over and snatched up his spear. Then, uttering the Asi death promise, he leaped up onto the ridge of the huge wing and climbed up until he stood on the shining armour of Geraragua's neck. There he poised for what seemed an eternal moment and below on the ground half of the Asi watched him with their hearts in their mouths while others turned their eyes away. Kobel shifted his feet for a firmer grip, the terrible head turned beside him and a furious eye opened. At that moment, in a lightning stab driven by pain and rage, Kobel thrust his spear deep into Geraragua's eye and pierced it to the very root.

Geraragua gave a gurgling roar. In his dying fury he flung Kobel and Meromo high into the air and Tajewo was spewed from his mouth in a fountain of blood. Then the enormous head sank to the ground and slowly the life seeped out of Geraragua.

A hush fell. Hesitatingly, little groups of Asi came closer, halting just clear of the great carcass. First a tentative spear thrust here and there and then, suddenly, cries of rejoicing as the little people swarmed forward to stare at the fallen horror that had haunted them so long.

But Gurum was aware of the price they had paid. He and the old warriors were clustering round Tajewo and Meromo and Kobel, who lay bloodied and unmoving. Presently Meromo groaned, staggered to his feet and then sat down again, stunned by his fall. Kobel sat up, bleeding but looking for his spear. When he saw that it was still stuck in Geraragua's eye, he struggled to his feet and went to retrieve it.

But Tajewo was lying on the ground where he had fallen and his eyes were closed. Gurum bent over him. 'He breathes, just a little,' he said. 'Quickly, bring the hide stretcher and take him to Mother Kinya.'

While the bearers shouldered their burdens of the wounded, shouts of victory began to ring out as the little warriors climbed over the huge carcass, reclaiming nets, arrows and spears and cutting off strips of black and yellow hide with which to make arm circlets. A man who had taken part in the hunting of Geraragua would wear on his arm a band that would elicit the respect of his sons and grandsons and great-grandsons, for the hunting of Geraragua had surpassed all the hunts there had ever been on the slopes of Oldoinyo Oibor.

Then the sky darkened. From Njororuet and the Ol Gelene hills ragged clouds were gathering, clouds of rushing wings and screaming voices that sank down over Nairob valley. The faithful ravens had summoned the flesh-eaters of the mountain to feast off the carcass. But before the feasting began, an ancient raven hopped up and perched on the scaly ridge over Geraragua's left eye. In the solemn, croaking tones of an elder, he imparted to the feathered throng a message from Mother Kinya. Only old Gurum understood his talk and he listened attentively as the raven told the winged folk about a stone that Geraragua had eaten, a stone as bright as the Morning Star. Somewhere in the carcass it was lodged, and though they were invited to feast upon the flesh until the bones were picked clean, the stone was to be brought to Mother Kinya and given into her hands alone. When the old croaker had spoken, Gurum nodded, well content, and followed his warriors home. Geraragua's carcass was left to the birds of the mountain, with the exception of a brown dog who had wisely watched the battle from the safety of a porcupine's lair and who now nipped in among the raucous feasters to scavenge on his own account.

The tired but exultant warriors came home to the village clearing to find a swarm of women round the common

86

fire. Pots were steaming over the coals and under the stern eye of Mother Kinya wives, sisters and daughters were preparing potions and compresses. And now men who only an hour ago had leaped and shouted in the heat of battle had to bow before the commands of healers and submit without flinching to the painful ministrations of their womenfolk.

Then the grievously wounded were carried home. Mother Kinya herself hurried over to them to exert all the power of her healing art upon the still bodies of Kapasiso, Kamek and Nandet, and Tajewo. Their wounds were cleansed and their heads gently supported as they were made to drink potions that would ease pain and induce healing sleep.

Kobel had to sit still while his scolding sisters cleansed the long wounds on his back. He gripped his tall spear in clenched hands and stared manfully ahead while Meromo, who had sustained only a few gashes, stood looking on.

'There is nothing like a fine scar, my kinsman,' he murmured, 'to remind a warrior that clear thinking and loyalty to battle plans are better than a desire for revenge.' Kobel shot him a fierce, proud glance and then bit on his lips so that no woman should elicit a whimper of pain from one who had given the death blow to Geraragua. And the hard, bloodied spear in his hands made the burning pain in his back seem a small and distant thing.

Presently Tajewo was borne away on a soothing river of sleep and forgetfulness, but Mother Kinya bent over Kapasiso with an anxious frown, for Kapasiso was still bleeding from the mouth and that was a bad thing. His wife sat keening beside him and suddenly the sound made Kinya angry. 'Go and gather those warriors,' she said, 'tell them to come and sing a praise song to this man who stood up alone and bore the brunt of the buffalo charge. This is what the spirit of Kapasiso needs, not the howling of a woman in his ears.'

When the weeping woman approached the Great Fire the crowd parted and the warriors who were recounting their exploits fell silent and listened to Kinya's request. Those who had been lucky in battle remembered how they owed their victory in great measure to the one man who had stood alone to divide the rushing herd. There was a thoughtful pause and then a young man took a little hide drum and gripped it between his knees, patting it softly until its rhythm drew the men together and rising up and surrounding the little huddled figure of Kapasiso, they began to sing. Gurum's deep voice was echoed by the strong clear voices of the men and, like the smoke of the Great Fire, a song of praise and thanksgiving rose up for Kapasiso. The song became a dance and as the westering sun shone into the clearing even the children lifted joyful little arms as the clans of Galuma celebrated the hunting of Geraragua and the noble deeds of Kapasiso, of Kamek and Nandet, of Tajewo, Meromo and Kobel.

At twilight a new Calling went out from the ironwood tree and news of the victory was made known to the clans of the high ridges. The next day, while the warriors lay and slept, little clan groups arrived, one after another, glad and anxious together lest a father or son lay wounded. Honey beer was passed from hand to hand, bushbuck meat sizzled on skewers and praise songs were made, then, that would be sung for generations.

Only Kinya and her helpers never rested. The wounded needed constant care and Kapasiso still hovered on the brink of the next world. In the moments snatched from nursing others, Kinya would sit beside Konyok, who had gone where the sound of her voice no longer reached him.

She knew that he was dying. Two days passed and then a third, but still Kinya waited in vain for a bird to come.

On the fourth day, in the weary twilight, she sat leaning against her hut wall to rest a few moments. As her head nodded and her old eyes began to close, a small bedraggled falcon flew into the clearing. It perched on a branch, peering among the huts as if looking for someone and gave a plaintive call. Mother Kinya looked up and saw it. She held out her arms in answer and the falcon swooped from the tree. For a moment it hovered and then into her cupped hands it dropped a bright stone.

'Ah,' said Kinya. 'At last! It is done. Thank you, little one.'

The bird rested gratefully on her wrist, for it was tired from days of foraging, pecked and trampled between the teeth of Geraragua, poking into corners too deep to be favoured by larger birds. Wedged at the very back of the lower jaw it had found the stone. Mother Kinya, whom no bird feared, stroked the grey head and spread a gift of dried termites in the palm of her hand.

When the falcon had flown away Kinya held up the stone and stared at it. Indeed, it was a tear. Clear as water from a mountain spring and yet glowing with a warm light. 'To think that our first mother held this in her hands at the gate of Paradise,' she whispered. 'If only Konyok knew...'

She rose and went in quietly to where the old man lay. 'Old Father,' she murmured, 'Geraragua lies dead and your son Kobel gave him the death thrust. Kibwere, our beloved, is avenged and the Stone of Naiterogop has been found. It has come too late for your eyes to see, but I lay it here on your breast so that you may feel it before you leave us for ever.' Then, worn out with work and with waiting, Kinya fell asleep.

In the hour that comes before dawn, when even the

feasters lie sleeping beside the embers, when the light of the Morning Star shines alone, Kinya dreamed that Konyok was calling her. She answered him fearfully, wondering whether his spirit called to her before departing to the world of shades. In her dream she searched for his face, stretching out her arms. But again he called her and she woke suddenly, for Konyok's voice was coming not from a dream, but from beside her in the hut. 'Is there no one round here to bring a thirsty man water?' he grumbled. 'Do the sick and old have to die in this place for lack of some honey beer and a little roast meat?'

Kinya ran stumbling for a light and calling out for Kobel. Together they came and knelt beside the old man and the eyes that Konyok turned upon his kin were reproving but bird-bright. 'And why, son of mine, do you walk as if a pitstake has been rammed into you?' he asked.

Then amid tears and laughter, Kinya and Kobel welcomed Konyok back into the land of the living. Lifting the hide from his chest she saw how the gangrenous weals had begun to heal and how the heat had passed from Konyok's body. The stone lay on his breast and from it spread healing on all sides. Their cries had brought others to the doorway and Gurum and his warriors crowded in to welcome Father Konyok back from the dead. Kinya covered the old one over again, but the stone she took quietly out with her to lay upon the crushed and lacerated body of Kapasiso. And later upon the cracked ribs of Nandet and Tajewo. Before evening of the same day, they were sleeping without pain and the healing of the stone was seeping through them.

Kinya said nothing of the stone, but when Tajewo rose the next day she told him what the little falcon had brought. 'I am glad it is in your hands, Mother Kinya,' he said. 'Keep it safe until it is time for us to go.'

8   Into the kingdom of Kibo

When Konyok, supported by Gurum and Kobel, walked out of his hut, a shout of joy rose from the gathered clans and when the old man had settled beside the Great Fire, the hunting of Geraragua was rehearsed for him from beginning to end. The telling of it became one long celebration and even Kapasiso was able to sit up and imbibe something that was stronger than water.

At last, when the night breeze sifted the ashes from the village fire, Mother Kinya called Tajewo and Meromo to her hut alone. She reached into the folds of her cloak for a pouch that she held out to Tajewo. 'The Stone of Naiterogop,' she said. 'Take it. It is yours now.'

Tajewo laid the stone in his palm and gazed at it, glowing in the firelight like a tear of gold. 'To think that this has travelled so far down the years,' he murmured, 'that once it lay at the gate of Paradise.' He held it up against the firelight. 'Even though it has sojourned in the body of Geraragua it looks pure and undefiled.'

He gave it to Meromo who took it cautiously at first, as if he believed it might burn his fingers. 'It is wondrous,' he said, 'a fragment of the great star himself, yet small enough for a man to hold. It is bright, yet it is gentle.' He stared at it in awe for a time, gently turning it in his fingers while its radiance filled the hut with the colours of the rainbow. Then he sighed. 'It seems a great pity that this should fall into evil hands. If this stone turned a harmless lizard into the fearsome Geraragua, what do you suppose it will do in the grasp of Moloch?'

Kinya nodded. 'It is going to be very hard to give up this treasure so old and so pure to one whose only desire is evil. It's as if you lie between the two tusks of an elephant, my friends,' she mused. 'Both are dangerous. If you refuse to give up the stone to Moloch, he will feed your people to his crocodiles. Yet if you surrender the stone to him, his power will grow and spread its black webs far over Oldoinyo Oibor.'

Tajewo closed his hand round the stone. Had it come to this then; that after the hardships of the quest, after the battle with Geraragua, they were merely trapped between two evils, whatever they did?

'If only I knew how to choose,' he sighed. He looked up and found the wise old eyes of Kinya upon him and it suddenly came to him that maybe the decision was not his, after all. He opened his hand and held out the stone. 'I give this back to you, Mother. The tear was shed at the feet of the first woman and perhaps the wisdom needed for this choice is not a man's. I leave it to a daughter of Naiterogop to decide what must happen to the stone.'

There was a sharp exclamation from Meromo, who felt that no man should leave such a decision to a woman. But Tajewo sent him a stern glance and Meromo had learnt to respect that look. He sighed and turned his eyes to the old woman.

Kinya regarded Tajewo first with surprise, and then with respect. 'Very well,' she said. 'It would be a hard choice for any of us.' She took the stone and slipped it into the pouch under her cloak. 'Whoever made you Alaunoni among your age mates could read hearts, Tajewo,' she said. 'You have what only a strong man has – the courtesy to listen to a woman's thoughts. I do not know any more than you what should be done, but I shall try not to fail you.' She sat frowning thoughtfully and then she said, 'Go and sleep now. I shall hold counsel with those who see further than we do. Rest well.'

The men went over to Kobel's hut to sleep, but Mother Kinya sat and gazed into the embers of her fire for a long time. Then she rose and wrapped her cloak round her and took up her staff. No one but the wood owl saw her solitary figure pass into the shadows of the forest.

Some time later she emerged on a path that climbed to the kranses of Teldeg. She came at last to sit upon a head of rock that faced east towards Kibo. There, with a prayer in her heart, she lifted up the stone to where the Morning Star hung in the heavens, alone and very clear, for the night was hovering on the brink of dawn.

When the first glimmer of light seeped into the eastern sky, the great star began to fade and Kinya hurried home. Once or twice she stumbled in her haste and the sound of her staff on the dry ground was full of purpose. 'It surprises me, I must admit,' she muttered. 'Yet, perhaps after all, I should not be surprised. They'll not have had much sleep tonight … but Kobel and I shall get the packing done first …'

Kobel started up, his sleep broken by a persistent tugging at his left earlobe. His mother was bending over him 'Kobel,' she whispered, 'come to my hut, quickly, but do not wake the others.' Drunk with sleep, Kobel followed her and leaned yawning against the doorway. Kinya was bending over the pots and baskets in her larder. 'You must be gone before sunrise, Kobel,' she said, 'with Tajewo and Meromo. You must take them right up to the wings of Kibo and there you must leave the tear of the Morning Star.'

'Mother … they have pledged the stone to Moloch! What will happen to their people if they return empty-handed?'

'That I do not know,' Kinya was scooping up roots from a covered pot. 'All I know is that the stone must be taken. I was not told what would happen after that.'

'But... you can't expect... what if...?'

'Kobel,' Kinya straightened up and pressed a rolled hide and a length of thong into his hands, 'you must do as I tell you, for the order is not mine. There is no time to lose. In my reckoning the journey will take several days, if the weather is kind – and you know well it's the season for mountain storms. Unless you go with them they will die before they ever reach the wings of Kibo. Now go and fetch those greased hides your father uses when he travels up high. And bring the pot of fat and the dried honey – and the jackal-skins and caps. No, there isn't time to argue. These roots must be pounded and I must find the thongs I cured from the buck hide you brought me...' She turned her back on Kobel and from sheer astonishment he was dumb. Wiping the sleep out of his eyes he went to find the hides and when he came back Kinya was heaping gear into piles – one large pile for her son and two smaller ones.

The sun was almost up when she sent Kobel to wake Tajewo and Meromo. They came and stood before her, heavy-eyed with sleep. Kinya held out a soft little bag and pressed it into Tajewo's hands, clasping them in her own for a moment. 'You must go now,' she said. 'I held counsel last night, on the heights of Teldeg. I lifted up the tear, beseeching the Morning Star to show me his heart in this matter. And it came to me, in a small voice as if he who is so far was close beside me, that what must be done is to take the stone very high, where the wings of Kibo brood above the world. There it must rest, given into the keeping of Kibo, beyond the grasp of men. And I think you must leave quickly, for it is a hard journey.'

'And what of Moloch – what of my people when I return empty-handed?' Tajewo's voice was hoarse with alarm.

Kinya regarded him steadily and in her old, seamed face Tajewo read a strange and fearless certainty. She laid her hand on his arm. 'I cannot say what is in the mind of the Morning Star, Tajewo. I am certain of one thing only – that this is his wish. And in my heart I know this: if the Great One wept for the sorrow of Naiterogop, he will be mindful of her daughters and sons.'

She looked at their dismayed faces and suddenly smiled. 'Plainsmen,' she said, 'in the great wide lands of the Naro-kem you can climb a little hillock and see in all directions. You can see where you are going and how far it is. But we of the mountains, when we travel, all we can see is the next hill, while the summit of the mountain hides far beyond. Now you must walk trustingly, as we of the mountain do. Climb as far as the next hill and there you will see the path ahead. Go now, as fast as you can. And remember that my Kobel has been to the very feet of Kibo and has returned. Trust him.'

Tajewo slipped the thong of the pouch over his neck and turned away to where Meromo held out a thick cloak of colobus fur to him. They shouldered the bundles Kinya had made while Kobel bent and heaved a large pack of provisions onto his back and drew the wide leather strap down over his forehead. He braced himself against his staff, slipped his quiver and bow over his left shoulder and turned and strode out of the clearing. Silently, like reluctant children sent off on a task they would rather not perform, they turned one last time to look at Kinya standing straight and assured beside the ashes of the village fire. She lifted her hand and waved them on and they turned and set their feet on the path, following Kobel into the gloom of the forest.

Shrouds of cold mist dripped from the leaves and they walked in silence until the trees thinned and they passed out of the forest into the high grasslands. They stood for a moment in the first rays of the rising sun to catch their breath and from the twisted branches of a giant heath tree the song of a bird rang out. Kobel pursed his lips and whistled an answer to the small bright voice. Meromo remembered an old fragment of song that the herdboys of Maasai used to sing as they led their cattle out to graze in the dew-bright mornings and as he began to sing they found their way up the steep and desolate hills with springing steps. They took a small grey path that twisted endlessly up towards the grim crags known as the Teeth of Shira. In spite of his heavy load Kobel walked faster than the plainsmen and he would stop now and then and look back, waiting for them. Meromo smiled at Tajewo, remembering a time, long ago, when they too had climbed a mountain with young and willing feet.

As the day wore on they had need of that memory, for soon the forests of Galuma fell behind them and above them rose the pitiless crags that shut out any glimpse of Kibo. Soon they were climbing on all fours, clutching at the polls of sharp, dry grass and heaving themselves up the narrow way between the lowering buttresses of rock. When at last they dropped exhausted on the summit of Shira the sun was high in the sky.

Here, for a little while, Kobel was merciful. He brought them water from a spring and let them lie stretched in the shade of an ancient twisted heath tree. Then he pointed north west. 'Look!' he said, 'look down on Atum Oldok. See where the river plunges over the falls into the pool. To think that Geraragua will never fly out again from his perch to terrorise the clans of Galuma!'

But soon Kobel was on his feet again, looking carefully at the sun. 'We must be getting on,' he said.

For a while they walked easily along a mountain saddle going east. Then the path climbed steeply again and they traversed sharp black shales interspersed with tough grasses. As the day wore on Tajewo and Meromo sank more often into the grass to rest while Kobel would stand impatiently beside them, urging them on. He seemed worried and would scan the eastern sky under his hand, often holding up a blade of grass to test the wind. Tajewo and Meromo were too tired to care about the wind. Every twenty paces they had to stop and catch their breath. Their ribs ached and their lungs seemed to be on fire. They often staggered from dizziness and there was a shrill singing in their ears. Kobel offered them slivers of dried meat and crumbs of the brown dry honey, but after only a mouthful or two their stomachs felt as tight as the cow's bladders that children blow up as footballs and nausea made them turn their faces to the earth and retch. Kobel would coax them gently but inexorably to their feet and lead them on. They looked at him with envying and resentful eyes.

'I don't know whether I love or hate the young wretch,' muttered Meromo, watching him stride so easily ahead, bent under his great load of jackal skins and provisions, topped by a bundle of heath-tree branches. 'But it is well for us that Kobel has the heart and lungs of an eagle. '

Tajewo nodded wearily, all his strength absorbed in putting one foot in front of the other, in willing himself to take the next painful step up the endless, stony path. 'If today is as bad as this, what will it be like when we climb to the feet of Kibo?' was all he could say. They both glanced up to the white arc that still seemed as distant and remote as when they had first left the forest. The sun overhead became so fierce that when an east wind came, pressing flat the grasses and tugging their cloaks, they welcomed it. But Kobel was frowning at a kaross of grey cloud spreading over the horizon. 'An east wind at this season is a wind of storm,' he said. 'We must hurry if we're to reach the cave of Engor before dark.'

All afternoon they trudged while the grey clouds massed, and the only sounds they heard were the croak of ravens and the whining of the east wind. At last they came to a shallow ravine where Kobel suddenly threw down his pack. 'We'll rest here,' he said and gave them water to drink; and while they lay back gratefully he began to cut swathes of long rough grass and stuff them into his pack.

'What's that for?' asked Meromo.

'Tonight I shall kindle our night-fire with it,' said Kobel, 'soon we'll come to the place where the grass ends and the hard mountain bushes begin and when we sleep under the rocks of Engor we'll be glad of a fire. Also, we shall need the grass for our feet.'

Meromo laughed weakly. 'Surely we shall fall over our feet if we go shod in grass?'

Kobel only grinned and went on cutting thick swathes. 'At least we shall have feet to fall over.'

'What are you telling me!' Meromo sat up and stared at him. 'Surely those stories about feet being eaten by the mountain are not true?'

'I haven't seen it myself, but I believe my father,' Kobel replied. 'It has not happened for a long time, but when my father was young there was a man who went up to the heights, for he wanted to speak to Kibo – he was mad, they say – and he found Kibo and lived. But when he returned he could hardly see and the toes of his feet turned black and decayed. They say his sight came back after a while, but no one has ever seen toes grow again.'

'Huh!' said Meromo, but behind his disbelieving grunt Kobel sensed consternation.

'So now, when we Asi have to go into the high country, we make shoes of greased hyrax skin padded with grass to keep the cold from gnawing at our feet.' When he had shoved the last handfuls into his pack he stowed his knife. Then he took a sip of water and stood up and heaved his pack onto his back and they rose and followed him. Though the sun still shone, it was as if they no longer felt its heat for the wind was colder now and it came roaring down from the heights in the east, pouring the cold breath of high snows over them. Tajewo and Meromo staggered and sometimes fell to their knees under its onslaught. The kaross of cloud gathered dark around them, torn apart for a brief while to reveal the fiery red of the setting sun. No one spoke anymore, for words were swept away by the howling wind. They staggered from one stony foothold to the next and they became aware that what had sounded like the thudding of drums was the desperate beating of their own hearts.

Darkness swooped upon them with monstrous wings and they barely saw the tumbled mass of rock beneath the buttress of Monya where Kobel stood and beckoned. They stumbled over to him and found themselves at the mouth of a cave, half blocked with fallen boulders. Here, suddenly, they passed out of the screaming wind into shelter and sank down in utter weariness. Before long, flames flickered up where Kobel crouched over a pile of grass and heath branches. Though they could do no more than lie with heaving chests and watch him, never had the two men felt a deeper gratitude than they felt then for the calm and me-ticulous preparations that Kobel was making for the long, cold night ahead.

'Son of Konyok,' muttered Meromo from cracked lips, 'without you these bones of mine would be lying on the mountainside, soon to be picked by the ravens of Kibo.'

Kobel glanced up and smiled, but as he pulled the jackal skins from his pack and began to make rough beds, close together and close to the small fire, he wore a preoccupied frown. Now and then he stopped and listened carefully to the voice of the wind that often rose to a high shriek among the rocks of Monya. 'The wind is bringing a storm on its wings,' he said presently. 'But I cannot tell yet whether it will bring snow or only ice rain. Nor how long it will last.' Then he turned back to the fire and began to pack stones closely round it, finally balancing on top of them a pot of water. When tendrils of steam began to rise he dropped into it some of the pounded roots that Kinya had packed. An aromatic steam filled the cavern and presently Kobel dipped small gourd scoops into the pot and gave the exhausted and sickened men a brew that they could drink without retching. It warmed their shaking bodies and cleared their minds, and when Kobel drew out dried meat and honey for their supper they found that they could eat and that they were hungry.

As their heavy eyelids drooped they were roused by Kobel packing the remaining hides and grass tightly round them while the stones heated by the fire were laid against their bodies. The last thing they were aware of was the figure of their young guide crouched against the entrance of the cave as he piled up stones to keep out the freezing fingers of the wind.

Yet, despite Kobel's precautions, the night seemed endless. Their first sleep of exhaustion passed into uneasy dreams and restless turning to escape the icy cold that seeped from the cavern walls and through cloaks and furs. All night long the wind buffeted the rocks of Monya, sending shales sliding and boulders grinding down from the heights. Several times Meromo started up out of a nightmare of a dark beast that prowled the mountaintop after them. Tajewo lay still and frozen by a dream of desolation in which he hung, powerless and undecided, between the cold sky and dark earth, far from all help while his people called to him in vain from afar. Kobel dozed fitfully, dreaming in snatches of the perilous climb ahead and of the sliding screes in the dark crater below Kibo. Several times he woke to stir the dying embers and revive the fire with heath bushes. It was only the golden flame of the hearth fire that kept him from a mad desire to run out into the howling night, down back to the forest and away from Oldoinyo Oibor. A flight that he well knew would bring a sure death from exposure or a fall down the crags of Shira.

A faint grey gleam woke Kobel. He crept from his bed and crawled stiffly over to the piled stones at the cave opening and removing one, peered out into flying snow. A deep white cloak had been laid over the mountain, covering the ground with icy softness. Kobel replaced the stone and crouched, frowning. The worst had happened. The coming of the thick snow would make the going hard – they could easily lose their way across the screes and the snow would clog their feet, slowing every step.

He sighed and took an armful of branches and fed the fire, replacing on a ring of stones the pot of root infusion. If he had to wake Tajewo and Meromo with bad news, at least there would be a hot brew to warm them before they began the battle towards the heights. When the aroma woke the sleeping men he fed them with meat and honey and told them of the snow.

'Baridi, the great white cold, has come. We will be walking into the teeth of a cruel wind and the going will be hard and dangerous,' he said.

Yet when Tajewo and Meromo stumbled out of the cave into the deep white drifts, they couldn't help scooping up handfuls of glittering snow, marvelling at its beauty, laughing like children as they watched it turn to water in the warmth of their palms. But Kobel pointed to the high slopes in the east and his face was sober: 'There are two days' walking before we may stand before Kibo. Before night comes we shall hate the snow.'

All the same, as they bound their feet with grass overshod with greased hide tied firmly with thongs, and dragged their packs from the cave, their hearts lifted at the beauty of the snow, wind-driven over shining slopes. Then, shading their eyes against the dazzle, they leaned forward over their staves and set out towards the heights of Kibo.

However, as the hours passed the beauty became a torture. The dazzling whiteness began to make their eyes ache and water. Strange shapes and shifting colours clouded their vision. Every ten paces they stopped to rest and the singing in their ears grew louder and dizziness and sickness overcame them. After midday the wind sprang up again, flinging sleet in their faces. Kobel, his anxious eye on the progress of the sun passing like a ghostly white ball behind flying clouds, let them pause just long enough to eat a mouthful of honey before he forced them on.

As darkness fell the fury of the storm was unleashed with driving hail. Kobel dragged the staggering plainsmen into the shelter of a small crag. And there, in a cleft scarcely out of reach of the screaming wind, they crouched, huddled between rock walls for the long night. Sleep came in short snatches between the howling of the wind and snow hurled upon them, until the cloak over their heads was heavy with snow and had to be shaken and replaced. The cold crept from their feet into their cramped legs and bodies and Kobel forced the older men to stand up and stamp their feet until they collapsed from weariness.

Tajewo was beyond thinking but bad dreams flitted like bats through the cave of his mind. He seemed to see some dark, subtle harm winding itself round his Loiyan, but it was in no form that he could name. And once, fleetingly, he saw the face of Natana Ole Kerewa, as it were, a long way off, speaking to him in words he could not hear. Only a sense that for a moment he was there.

The cruel half-light of dawn found Kobel pulling them to their feet. Without words he bound their fur cloaks firm-ly to their bodies and then, leaving the packs in the rocky gully, he took his staff and led them up into a wilderness of black rock, bitter wind and flying snow.

After some hours of painful trudging, the ground on their left fell away in a glistening black scree and through the swirling snow they glimpsed the depths of the crater Mrija, lying like the treacherous cone of an ant-lion. A fall into Mrija meant no return. The path was narrow between the fall and boulders on the right. Their breath came in sobs as they stumbled on, and once Meromo lost his foot-ing and slid down into the loose shingle of Mrija. Kobel turned and grasped his staff and, lying in the path, hauled him up again. After this he bound their staves to their right arms with thongs and then in his right hand he took Tajewo's staff and Tajewo took Meromo's staff in his left hand and so they staggered on, pulled and guided by the steadfast strength of Kobel. The hours passed as slowly as their dragging footsteps and all their thought and will were bent on only one thing, which was to put one foot in front of the other and not to stop. They knew that if they stopped, they would never rise to go on again.

The world was lost to them in a twilight of mist and sharp sleet. They did not notice the gradual change at first but eventually it came to them that the voice of the wind had quietened, that ahead of them was a lightness, a peace, a sheltering place where the wind could not come. The snow was no longer blown into their faces but was falling slowly, white and gentle. All about them was a white mist through which something shone with a pale green shining. Then they realised that the light came from gleaming wings of ice that rose to unfathomable heights somewhere ahead of them.

'Kibo!' Kobel whispered between cracked lips. 'The wings of Kibo!'

It was then that Tajewo fell headlong in the snow, bringing Meromo down with him. He struggled for a moment to rise and then sank into a deep sleep. In vain Kobel tugged at him and shook him. Time was passing and they must return to the rock shelter before night fell. If they did not reach it they would die during the night. What should he do? He shook Meromo violently but he lay as limp as a dead man. Yet the task they had come to do had to be done. Kobel stooped and slipped the pouch thong over Tajewo's head. He reached into it and brought out the stone. Then, grasping it to his heart, he walked away into the softly falling snow, towards the shining wings in the light ahead.

When they asked him, later, what he had seen at the feet of Kibo he never quite found words for it. He found himself walking into light and yet more light and a sense of Someone who held about him a cloak of shifting green brightness. Someone who, great as the mountain, was yet mindful of one who was as small as a river fly at his feet. Kobel's strength was all but gone as he walked forward into the quiet, light place until the snow was too deep for him to go any further. He laid the stone in the snow before the Shining One and then walked away backwards until he tripped over his own staff and fell into the snow beside Tajewo and Meromo.

For some time Kobel lay where he had fallen. A sense of peace passed into him. It had been done. What would happen now none of them knew. They had accomplished what they had been told to do. The stone lay in the safekeeping of Kibo. Now their last shreds of strength would be given to getting back down Oldoinyo Oibor without breaking their legs or slithering down the screes of Mrija.

He reached out for his staff but instead of wood he grasped something cold, smooth and rope-like. He sat up quickly and stared. He was holding a long, silver-white skein that lay on the snow beside his footprints. It was several times the length of a man and it gleamed with the same unearthly ice-green of the wings of Kibo.

'Tajewo – Tajewo, Meromo!'

Kobel's hoarse, excited cries roused them at last from their stupor. They sat up and stared at the shining thong in Kobel's hands, as smooth as the white hair of some giant. It was as soft as the down on an owl's breast, yet it gleamed like ice and was stronger than any thong cured by men. In wonder they ran their hands over it. At last Tajewo recollected himself and muttered, 'Where is the stone – what happened?'

'It is done,' said Kobel. 'You fell asleep here and nothing could move you. So I took the stone – look, the pouch is empty. I went until I could go no further and laid it – there.'

Tajewo looked to where he pointed into the shining mist and glimpsed the distant shimmer of great wings. Then he nodded and sighed, 'My son, my strength failed and you did well. Without you we would not have done what we set out to do. And this … this … rope?'

'I found it lying here beside me in the snow. I fell coming back, and there it was.'

'Then it must be meant for us,' said Tajewo. 'It's strange – I feel as if I've slept for a day and a night, and I'm the better for it. I feel strong again – strong enough to face the journey back. Let us go now, for as you have said, it is done.'

Tajewo found that when he rolled up the strange cold rope it fitted easily into the pouch that had carried the stone. When he had stowed it round his neck, he slowly turned his face away from the shining mist and followed Kobel and Meromo down the mountain.

9 Loiyan and the black leopard

As Meromo and Tajewo struggled against the awesome powers of wind and snow on the heights of Kibo, their people in the cave of Nalankeng were battling with the fear in their hearts. They did not know why they had been thrown into the dark cavern. Their men had been taken from them, leaving them with the young children and their aged parents. And why did no one come to them? Why did their captor not reveal himself, and where were Tajewo, Meromo, Kidoni and Naikosiai? Fear and uncertainty bred bad dreams in the darkness that eroded their hope and courage. They glimpsed daylight for only a few moments when Moloch's servants rolled away the stone from the entrance and tossed in just enough fodder to keep the cattle alive. At midday a narrow beam of sunlight shone through a crack in the cavern roof and reminded them of the world outside where people walked under the wide sky and felt the wind on their faces.

But they were the proud people of the Narokem and to keep up their spirits they worked every day as they had always done. They tended the herds and cleaned and smoked the long gourds for milking. They repaired torn cloaks and broken sandals, singing the old toil songs that had gladdened the work of generations. At night the old people told fireside tales, and as they listened they felt, just for that time, that they were in the old, loved places under the fields of the stars. Then they would roll their cloaks round them and, with their feet towards the fire, lie down to sleep.

Only Loiyan sat alone and wakeful, after the others had fallen asleep, waiting for a glimpse of the strange little bat. Sometimes he flitted from some crack in the depths of the cave and circled her head, only to disappear again. 'Perhaps he comes to tell me that we are not forgotten,' she mused. 'I wonder – who is this woman with the pot that sends him to me?' Once or twice Impimpi let fall a pod or a fragment of bark on which some tiny drawing was scratched of men with spears and other quaint beings over which Loiyan pondered, but whose meaning she could not grasp.

In her lonely vigils she roamed the cave and she filled the water pots from the cold stream that flowed from tumbled boulders into a pool. Most of all she liked to stare up at the crack in the ceiling through which she could see the stars and sometimes a fragment of the white moon.

It was during her night vigils, when even the loyal Nandi slept, that Loiyan became sure that she was being watched. She would peer anxiously into the gloom beyond the fire-light, but she could see nothing. Yet she felt a presence in the darkness, in the depths where the silent stream flowed – a presence that moved stealthily towards her and then withdrew again into the cavern's depths. Loiyan became afraid to sleep and would sit staring into the darkness, lest the watcher should come upon her unawares.

Nandi began to notice shadows under Loiyan's eyes and how she fell asleep now and then over her daily tasks. 'Sister,' she said, 'you are tired. If you let worry eat up your sleep you will fall ill, and who will feed Lemeikoki then? Sleep like the rest of us, in trust. There is nothing we can do but wait.' She would pull Loiyan down beside her and lay her kind arm over her shoulders. Sometimes, then, Loiyan slept a little but later she would wake suddenly and, as if drawn by a strange call, she would rise and walk beyond the wavering firelight, towards the dark reaches of the cavern, and it was there that she first saw the eyes.

They were yellow eyes flecked with green, like those of a huge cat and they were moving, disappearing and then appearing again, circling closer. One night, as she sat alone near the stream, the eyes shone suddenly out of the shadows nearby and Loiyan froze as an enormous black leopard leaped over the stream and stood before her, lifting its muzzle in a snarl. She waited, frozen with terror, for its teeth to close on her neck. But the leopard did not spring. Instead it stared into her eyes and suddenly it ducked and sleeked its head against her shoulder. Loiyan's heart was thudding but she kept very still while the beast circled her several times. It rubbed its sleek body against her and then, with a long backward stare, it leaped away into the shadows.

In the nights that followed, the leopard returned, dallying longer beside her, paying court to Loiyan, trying to lure her down into the shadowed depths of the cave, beyond the stream. One night the little bat flew out and circled the cave but when it saw the leopard it darted away with a ragged swoop, so swift that Loiyan scarcely saw it. And Loiyan began to wonder. Why were the cattle not panicked by the leopard that prowled the cave each night? Usually the pacing of a leopard close by would send the bulls into a frenzy. And who had ever heard of a leopard that was blacker than night and greater than the greatest lions of Narokem? Was this dark beast a friend, sent perhaps by the woman who sent the bat? Or ... if not, then what power was weaving itself round her ... and why?

One night, as the leopard sleeked sinuously against her, Loiyan inched closer to the fire. She wished to look more carefully at her strange haunter. She lifted a burning branch and held it up and as the light fell upon him, the leopard turned and sprang away into the darkness. But for a brief moment the firelight threw a shadow against the wall – not the shadow of a leopard but of a tall man, leaping with outspread arms into the depths below. Loiyan's heart turned over in fear.

Under the thin curve of the waning moon, the dark river god paced restlessly over the Lolgoron. Ever since he had seen her praying at the riverside, Moloch had desired Loiyan, and when he had taken Tajewo's people he had wished to acquire her as much as to punish Tajewo for insulting Ndamathia. Even if Tajewo retrieved the Stone of Naiterogop, Moloch did not intend to relinquish this woman with skin the colour of wild honey. Two nights ago a hammerhead had flown from high upstream with news that the monster Geraragua had perished in a battle with the clans of Galuma. Moloch had smiled. If the old monster of Atum had indeed swallowed the stone and they had found it, then soon they would be on their way down to him, with triumph in their foolish little hearts. They imagined, no doubt, that he would keep his word and relinquish their families, including the beautiful Loiyan. They would soon realize that they were dealing with one whose power lifted him above the keeping of a pledge to mere human creatures. He would take the stone and keep the woman as well. He would let the people go – though a few plump cattle would not come amiss to placate his cold children … However, in order to provide a little amusement and to make it look as if the failure of honour were on their side entirely, it would be as well to see that Tajewo was delayed. If he were to return too late for the first night of the new moon then he would forfeit his wife. Moloch gave a low hiss and a dark form slid from the rocks of the krans to receive his instructions.

All the next day Loiyan pondered on the man-shadow that had leaped away from the firelight. Now she knew what her heart had intuited all along – the creature of the night that paid her court was a shape-changer, some spirit of the river valley who had her in his thrall. Who was he and what did he want of her?

When the great cat came again the next night and sleeked his head against her, purring and lying down beside her like some household pet, Loiyan was not surprised when, suddenly, the dark beast became a tall man who lay with his arms around her. She stifled her terror and allowed him to draw her to him with sweet words as he recounted his long desire for her, and how he had taken her people captive only in the hope of winning her love. If the beautiful Loiyan would become his bride, he promised, then her people would be free to return to their home on the plains and he would recompense Tajewo with a hundred head of cattle. Loiyan would become a queen of the great river on the mountain, the favoured one who would hold sway over his realm. He would deny her nothing and upon her forehead she would wear the Stone of Naiterogop as the sign of his favour.

Loiyan's heart became cold as she began to understand the danger that threatened her people. But her quick wits warned her that to show revulsion would not help her. She must disguise her feelings and, since the dark spirit had ensnared her people with guile, so she must weave her own deceptions in order to save them. She glanced up at the man with the cat's eyes and then smiled shyly, hanging her head like a maiden receiving the attentions of her first admirer. 'My lord flatters me,' she whispered. 'Surely such a high one cannot care for a simple girl who tends cattle on the plains?'

'The warmth of sun on golden water shines on your skin, daughter of the plains,' said Moloch, eyeing her with a greed that made Loiyan's heart convulse with fear. 'I value that warmth and the sweetness of a voice that runs like honey from a pressed comb.' With one last caress he left her and melted into the shadows. When she was sure he was gone, Loiyan crept back to the fire, but first she washed her hands in the stream.

Moloch had spoken the truth when he had avowed his lust for warmth and sweetness. He craved them indeed, for like a reptile he withered if he could not absorb the warmth of others as a snake that lies on sun-warmed rocks. One woman after another he had pursued and won, only to cast her away as she faded in his dark caverns, overcome by the coldness of his heart. He had promised each one power and possessions and they had perished slowly of loneliness.

After he had left her, Loiyan could not sleep. At last she woke Nandi and told her in whispers that it was Moloch himself who held them captive and that he wanted her as his wife. She told her too of the little bat that flew in to her with messages from some woman with a pot who seemed to know who they were and who knew of four men with spears on a dangerous quest. When she had poured out her tale, Loiyan fell asleep from exhaustion and relief but now it was Nandi who lay awake, staring wide-eyed into the darkness.

From the rock of Lolgoron shadowy figures streamed along the river shore. Moloch's henchman, the wicked Norongurr, was leading out a hunting band. Like a misbegotten form from some evil dream, he lifted his muzzle and sniffed the night air. Then he gave a long howl and slid into the forest with his followers behind him. They were carrying nets and spears and they made their way silently up the foothills to hunt the two men descending from the Galuma.

In the cave below, Nandi sat, gnawed by fear and too angry to sleep. Now she knew why Loiyan had sat staring fearfully into the shadows night after night. Nandi shuddered. They were the playthings of a wicked spirit – a group of women and children and defenceless old parents. What could they do against the power of Moloch? Alone, she knew, they could do nothing. But what about the woman with the bat...? She took a glowing branch from the fire and rose. 'If Loiyan does indeed receive a visitor from a woman with a pot – I hope it's not merely the dream of one whose fear is eating away her mind – then there must be a passageway along which he flies. And if the wings of a bat can flit along it, then maybe a woman, crawling on her belly, can go that way too...'

She crept over to a mass of tumbled boulders in a far corner of the cave and the flame on the branch flickered suddenly. 'Ah,' Nandi whispered, 'somewhere here... somewhere over here, the cave is breathing.' She clambered over the rocks until high up under the cave roof she saw soft white tendrils of mist. She raised the glowing branch and saw an opening in the rock just large enough for her to enter. Biting her lips in the fear that a plainswoman feels for dark and narrow places, Nandi crawled into the hole.

Holding the glowing branch in front of her, she dragged herself forward on her belly. In a few moments the mist that flowed down the crevice extinguished the burning tip of her torch. She had to grope her way forward in the dark, grasping at rough handholds in the rock to pull herself along. Soon the passageway began to slope steeply upwards. Several times it twisted and once Nandi found herself wedged in a bend, unable to go forward or back. For a terrible moment the breath left her body and her heart hammered in her terror of suffocation. She struggled like a wild thing in a snare, kicking herself forward with a desperation that sheared the skin off her legs and shoulders. Then she lay free once more, and sobbed with relief to feel space at her fingertips and cool air flowing gently over her face. Slowly and painfully she pulled herself along. At last there was a glimmer of golden light ahead and mist creeping soft and thick and, somewhere, an old voice singing. Gasping with relief, dishevelled and grey with dust, Nandi dragged herself out onto the floor of a cave.

The singing stopped. Out of the mist an old woman appeared with an owl on her shoulder. She gave a little exclamation of surprise, 'Ooh – up through impimpi's passage! Child of my child, you are bleeding! All that way! Come and sit down. Yes, yes, over here. That's right...' Nandi was grasped by strong old hands and helped over to sit on grass piled against the cave wall. 'Child of my child, are you Loiyan, wife of Tajewo, of whom my Im pimpi brings me news each night?'

'No, Mother of my mother,' whispered Nandi. 'I am Nandi, wife of Meromo. But we share one heart, Loiyan and I, as do our husbands. I left her sleeping. She is worn out with fear, for Moloch has cast his net about her. And I sat thinking, for I couldn't sleep and it seemed that the only thing for me to do was to find you, for we do not know where to turn.'

'Well now,' Marumuruti's eyes widened in approval, 'it seems as if you are as good a friend to Loiyan as your husband is to Tajewo. You are wise, Nandi – and very courageous. Not many would have braved the tunnel from the cave of Nalankeng. I am glad you have come – very glad. A great deal has happened since yesterday's sunrise and words spoken into your ear will serve better than a whole handful of scratchings on pods. But look at you. Bat droppings in your hair and blood on your legs! Pull that cloak around you against the cold. There, now. I have something that will restore you ...'

Marumuruti bustled off and presently returned with a gourd scoop of a hot, sweet-smelling broth. Nandi could not help staring at her remarkable hostess. 'Old Mother,' she whispered as she took the gourd, 'who are you?'

'I am Marumuruti, she who sends the mists along the river valleys,' said the ancient one. 'I have no love for Moloch, my daughter, and I am aware of the peril you are in. Your menfolk came to me in their hour of need and together we are working to undo the snares that Moloch has set for your people. But speak quietly, child, while I draw a cloak of silence around us.'

Once a dense fog had risen from her cauldron, Marumuruti pulled her stool over to sit beside Nandi. 'Child of my child,' she said, 'strange news has come to me from the high forests. The Stone of Naiterogop has been found – oh, but I'm forgetting! You know nothing of all that. Well, I shall have to begin at the beginning – no, that is too much to tell. Let me see ...'

As she murmured the tale of Moloch's bargain for the Stone of Naiterogop, Nandi's eyes grew wide. 'My daughter, brave deeds have been done which will yet be sung of. But the stone was destined to pass beyond the grasping hands of men and of Moloch. And that is good. No, do not be afraid. It would have been the worse for all of us if it had been brought here. It rests now where Kibo dwells high above the world. And, what is more, my wise old messenger brings me news of a gift – a gift in exchange, from Kibo himself. A strange gift – a single white hair which has the power to turn blood to ice and flesh to stone.' Marumuruti nodded and looked meaningfully at Nandi.

'But how can that help us?' cried Nandi.

Marumuruti placed her finger on the young woman's lips. 'Speak softly,' she whispered. 'These days even the forest has ears.'

'But if they return without the stone we shall all die!' Tears suddenly glimmered in Nandi's tired eyes. 'It will all have been in vain!'

'Oh no – not in the least! I have been plotting, child of my child. A little harmless planning is a weakness of mine!' A mischievous smile spread over Marumuruti's face and she poked Nandi gently with a gnarled finger. 'Now listen very carefully. You, Nandi, have shown courage beyond my expectations. You have braved the dark passage from Nalankeng to find me and now we can plot together. You will be the one to help me set a trap – a snare to catch one who sets traps for others. At this very moment the nets of Moloch are closing round Tajewo and Meromo as they come down through the forest.'

Nandi's eyes grew wide as Marumuruti recounted Moloch's betrayal of his pact with Tajewo. 'Then, either Tajewo must lose Loiyan – which will break his heart, or we in the cave must be thrown to the crocodiles of Lolmoloch!' she cried.

'Hush, girl, and listen carefully. I have not been idle, my daughter. We have one hope still. It is the love of Tajewo for

his son, Lemeikoki. Now, this is what must be done…'
Marumuruti spoke earnestly and presently the despair on
Nandi's face gave way to a look of cautious hope. 'Above all,
my child, you must insist that when Moloch comes for her
– and he will come soon, I think – Loiyan must take her
little son with her. On no account must she be parted from
him. I know that the old grandparents will weep and plead;
they will cry that she is taking their very life from them.
Loiyan must harden her heart. She must play the proud
bride, make herself beautiful and act the temptress with
Moloch, but she must not be parted from her child. Have
you remembered everything I have told you, Nandi? Now, I
fear you must hurry back, child of my child. Courage, girl,
courage! We shall meet again before the moon is full.'

When Nandi had wormed her way back into the tunnel,
Marumuruti sent Kovankuni off into the forest and returned to her cauldron. When the owl flew in again later
she bore news of an ambush in the forest, a valiant fight in
which several of Moloch's servants had been wounded, and
others bitten in the ankle. But the two gallant plainsmen
had been overpowered like beetles by driver ants. 'They
have them, Old Mother. They are trussed and hanging
from trees and Moloch's creatures harass them, pricking
them in places of indignity with the tips of their spears.
Hooooo! They are heartsore, Mother of Mists, and as bitter
as cornered cobras.'

'As long as Tajewo has not been robbed of a pouch…?'
whispered the old woman.

'No, he has it still, under his cloak,' murmured the owl.

'Good. That is all that matters. Now, like them and like
those in the caves below, we must wait, my Kovankuni; we
must wait for the new moon to rise…'

10   The new moon's rising

Below the krans of Lolgoron the river valley brooded in silence. Once, a heron croaked, roused by an old woman wreathed in mist passing beneath the fig trees on the river bank. Presently she stood still and, leaning on her stick, she stared up at the rock of Lolgoron. Like a marrowbone from a carcass, it seethed with the black swarms of Moloch's creatures. On the summit protruded the broken tooth of rock that was his seat.

Suddenly the swarms parted and Moloch himself stalked slowly out over Lolgoron to sit upon the stone seat from where he surveyed the reaches of his river. He held an ebony staff in his hand. Slowly the golden light of the after-noon drained from the valley and dusk fell. The silver crescent of the new moon rose over the hills and with a murmur that swelled like a river in flood the dark hordes on Lolgoron hailed her coming.

Moloch rose and lifted his staff. 'Ha!' he cried. 'Now the new moon hangs in the sky. At any moment the gallant plainsmen will appear, bringing a ransom for their people.'

Time passed and the crescent of the new moon shone brightly over the river, but there was no sign of Tajewo and Meromo. At last Moloch rose and called their names loud-ly so that his voice echoed from the kranses. As he expected, there was no answer and cold laughter spread among his followers. He waited with exaggerated patience until the moon had passed into the west behind the foothills. Then he uttered a harsh cry of triumph and smote the rocks of the krans with his staff: 'I struck a bargain with the men of

the Narokem!' he declared. 'They promised to be here on
the night of the new moon's birth. They have not come –
no doubt they are carousing in the forest!' He paused
amidst mocking laughter. 'Therefore they must pay a forfeit to me. I will be magnanimous. If they come tomorrow,
I shall still receive them and I will grant them a second
chance to redeem their people. Nonetheless, it will be my
right to exact my price for this favour.' A roar of acclama-
tion echoed his words while his creatures swarmed down
from Lolgoron into the caverns below.

'You loathsome old spider,' muttered the Mother of
Mists making her way back to her cave, 'you spinner of evil
webs. May you be bound by a web that is stronger still.'

In the cavern of Nalankeng the old women were telling
stories in the meagre firelight as they did every night. But in
the shadows beyond, Loiyan and Nandi wandered restlessly
and only little Koki sitting on his grandmother's lap saw how
Nandi took off her gleaming copper bracelets and slid them
onto Loiyan's arms. Then she draped her bright beadware
over Loiyan's shoulders until she stood adorned, looking as
tall, proud and beautiful as the wife of a very great chief.

High in the forest Meromo and Tajewo hung from an ironwood tree like insects in a web. There had been a short and
bitter battle when they had walked into Norongurr's
ambush but they had been hopelessly outnumbered. Now
they had to bear the mockery of their captors who sat by
their watch fires, roasting meat and darting over from time
to time to tease their captives with spear thrusts. But no
mockery was equal in bitterness to the knowledge that they

had failed to meet Moloch on the night of the new moon's rising.

Tajewo was terrified that if he fell asleep, the pouch round his neck would be stolen. He wrestled with the harsh meshes of the net until he had crossed his arms over his chest and his right hand clenched his knife. In despair he watched the new moon rise in the evening sky. When its light was eclipsed behind the forest ridges he fell into exhausted sleep.

Meromo saw Tajewo's eyes close and knew he had to remain vigilant for both of them. He kept himself awake by digging into his hand with his knife and presently he found comfort in remembering how they had taken leave of Konyok, Kinya and Kobel in the forest of Galuma. The Asi had wept openly as they had set off from the village clearing and old men, even the doughty Kapasiso, recovered from his wounds, had come forward with bracelets of Geraragua's hide, gifts from one warrior to another. With tears running down his face, Kapasiso had thrust a circlet onto Meromo's arm and had called him a brother of the high ridges forever.

Konyok, standing proudly upright with Gurum and Kinya beside him, had sent the blessing of the Forest Spirit with them and Kobel had accompanied them to the fig tree. As he stood there in the morning sunlight, his hand raised in farewell, he had asked, 'Shall I see you again, kinsmen of Narokem?' and Tajewo had turned and said, 'Most surely, son of my right arm! We will not let the years be long!' And Kobel had stayed looking after them until the forest had swallowed them from his sight...

Meromo woke suddenly and blinked. A shaft of sunlight was hot on his skin. Silence hung over the forest, broken only by the rustle of a thrush scratching among fallen leaves. That was all. The clearing was empty. Moloch's bullies had gone and only dead embers and crushed undergrowth showed where they had revelled. Still, he peered suspiciously among the dark trees half expecting to see the glint of spears until Moipu trotted into the clearing. He wagged his tail, whined at his master and then sat down and scratched.

'Well, the dog would not sit scratching his fleas if those creatures of Moloch were nearby,' Meromo muttered. Stiffly he turned and peered over at his sleeping companion. 'Tajewo!' he called. 'Tajewo – wake up! They've gone!'

Tajewo's first thought was for the pouch round his neck. Yes, it was there still beneath his arms. But he felt strangely cold and too numb to move. Meromo was struggling with his knife to cut himself loose and when he had stumbled out of his net he had to cut Tajewo out of his snare and help him to his feet. Only slowly could they release his arms that were as cold as stone from the power of the white hair of Kibo. 'It's a good thing Mother Kinya thought to guard this cold rope with the thick pouch full of grass. Otherwise I think it would have frozen your heart by now,' muttered Meromo, rubbing the life back into Tajewo's stiff limbs.

Moipu had found a well-trodden path and they followed him down through the forest towards the river valley.

Stumbling along behind Meromo, as the cold sleepiness left him, Tajewo pondered over their strange release. 'Why do I still have the pouch, Meromo? If Moloch did not send his henchmen to rob me, then why did they capture us?'

'Perhaps he does not trust his minions,' said Meromo. 'It seems to me that he wants us to bring him what he supposes is the stone, but to arrive later than the appointed time.'

'So that we appear to have broken our pledge,' mumbled Tajewo.

'And if we have not fulfilled one of his conditions, then he does not have to keep to his side of the bargain,' finished Meromo. 'The snake!' he added, spitting loudly into the bushes. 'No doubt we'll know soon enough what it is he plans.' He glanced up. 'The sun's going behind the western ridges. We must hurry.'

They came down at last to the river valley and walked along the river bank to where the rock of Lolgoron rose black in the purple twilight. The day-old moon was shining above the hills. They looked up and saw the massed ranks of Moloch above them. As they approached Lolgoron, Moloch rose and with an imperious gesture of his arm he summoned them. They climbed the steep path that wound up the krans and the hostile eyes of Moloch's hordes glinted coldly at them as they passed. The dark spirit towered over them as a hooded cobra looms above his prey. As they approached they saw that behind him stood another figure. The light of the new moon shone upon swathes of gleaming jewelry, on the long neck and slanting eyes of Loiyan. They caught their breath, but Loiyan did not move. Her eyes were cast down and in her arms Lemeikoki lay sleeping. At that moment an arrow of doubt pierced Tajewo's heart. The face of his wife was as hard and still as carved stone.

'Well, plainsmen,' Moloch looked down at the two ragged and weary men with seeming courtesy but with malice glinting in the depths of his eyes. 'It seems that you have decided to observe our tryst, after all. But, as you see, the moon is already a day old. Did we not agree that you were to be here on the day of her first rising?'

'We did indeed,' Tajewo answered bitterly. 'For reasons of

your own, Moloch of Lolmoloch, we were delayed in the forest by a swarm of insects. Yet we have come all the same, for we have remembered the other part of this bargain.' He touched the pouch that hung from his neck.

For a moment Tajewo was aware of a seething lust within his tall opponent. Moloch's hand stirred, almost reaching out to grasp him and the pouch together. But Tajewo stood his ground. 'I would have it known,' he cried and his voice rang out suddenly in the dark gorge, a tired, human voice, 'I would have it known that in so far as we could, we have honoured our pledge. We have braved the heights of Kibo in order to redeem our people. We have gone where others have not had the courage to go – even those whose greed for power is great!'

Tajewo felt Moloch's anger then, but his eyes were on Loiyan, willing her to look at him for just one moment. Yet though he thought her eyes flickered towards him, her face was closed. Untouched, she would not plead on his behalf.

'I will be generous,' said Moloch, reining in his anger. 'You have fulfilled one half of your promise and therefore I shall grant you the lives of your people. I shall release them and you may leave the valley of Lolgoron tomorrow as the sun rises – you and your people and your cattle. But because you failed to return at the new moon I shall keep for myself your wife Loiyan.'

So this was the poison the spider had stored in his fangs! Rage burned in Tajewo's heart and he raised his spear shaft. But Meromo's fist closed like iron on his shoulder. 'No!' he hissed. 'No. Take care. This is not the time. Wait ... wait, my friend.' Tajewo shuddered. Once more he gazed at Loiyan, hoping for one glance from her eyes that belied Moloch's boast. But Loiyan stood turned to stone, staring beyond him in haughty silence.

'Then give me back my son!' Tajewo cried in his heart-break. 'Give me my only son and we shall leave.'

'My lord,' Loiyan moved then, sidling towards Moloch with the flattering looks of a maiden in love with a great warrior, 'the little man is right. What is his son to us? You will desire sons of your own blood. What use will you have for a little frog of the plains? Let me give him his son in return for the pouch that hangs round his neck. It is a small price to pay for the treasure my lord has sent for.'

Before Moloch could answer her, Loiyan glided forward. With nimble fingers she took the pouch from Tajewo and peered into it and a sly smile lit her lovely face. 'My lord,' she said, 'the treasure is yours at last. Let me conceal it in my bosom and bestow it upon you presently, as we feast together.' She thrust her sleeping child into Tajewo's arms. 'Take your son, plainsman, and leave us.' Tajewo took Lemeikoki from her and turned and walked down from Lolgoron, his heart in turmoil. As they left, darkness fell.

Moloch turned to gaze in triumph on the tall, graceful woman at his side. It was as if he had captured the silver moon herself, as if the most remote and beautiful inhab-itant of the night sky was now his own, his very own to grasp and hold for ever. And Loiyan, slipping the pouch deep under her clothing, lifted her smiling face up to her lover. Her arms slid invitingly over his and together they passed through the waiting hordes into the caverns below. Dull red torches lit the endless caverns of Moloch and the heartbeats of huge drums announced the marriage feast of Moloch and Loiyan.

As they entered the feast hall dancers leaped out of the shadows and they danced wildly as Moloch led his bride to the couch of black leopard skin where they were to recline together. When the gourds of fiery liquor were brought,

Loiyan held them up to her chief. With her own slim hands she picked out succulent morsels for him from the heaped platters. Moloch's eyes seldom left her to roam over the dancers spinning between the feast fires. And still Loiyan lifted the slender gourds to his lips, and laid her head upon his breast and slid her soft hands over his arms and face ...

Swift as the dancers' feet the hours fled. As the fires died and dancers sank to the ground, the eyelids of the revellers drooped and drumbeats slowed. Then Loiyan began to sing for her lord. A gentle, lilting song of a girl walking over the green plains of the Narokem, in search of a beautiful bull which she would draw home with a soft hide thong. She sang until Moloch's eyelids drooped and then she slid the pouch from under her cloak. Singing, she drew out the soft silver rope. Singing still, she knotted a noose while she caressed her lord, telling him to sleep deeply like the bull tethered safely in the cattle byre. As she sang she slipped the noose over Moloch's head and wound the cold rope about his arms and shoulders. Moloch felt only the softness of her hands and he smiled and closed his eyes. Loiyan's singing lulled him into deep sleep while she wove the shining coils round Moloch's limbs until even his feet were meshed with gleaming light. The light grew and the coldness of ice spread through the sleeping river lord. For one moment, as the cold seeped into his heart, he woke and his eyes opened in terror. But he was numb beyond moving and as Loiyan watched, Moloch of Lolmoloch turned slowly into cold grey stone. A sighing echo breathed through the caverns as Moloch died. His creatures died with him, withering like leaves borne away on a night breeze until only silence remained.

Loiyan ceased her singing. She rose and plucked off her finery. She threw the headbands and bracelets, the neck rings and the glistening beads to the floor. She cast away her cloak and, wearing only her hide dress, she walked out of the reeking caverns. She groped along stone passages till she came to the stairs leading out of the black maze. At last she stood on the height of Lolgoron as dawn was breaking. She breathed the cool air of the forest and looked up to where, clear and shining on the eastern horizon hung the Morning Star.

A figure huddled beside a boulder started up and with a cry of joy the faithful Nandi clasped her in welcoming arms. For a long moment Loiyan held Nandi to her, speechless with relief. 'It is over,' she said. 'Moloch is nothing but a grey stone and his people have faded with the mist.' She shuddered. 'I feel defiled. Let us go down to the river and bathe.'

As they stood washing in the shallows they heard the joyous barks of a dog. Moipu bounded out of the fig grove, greeting them with tail and tongue, and he was followed by an old woman trailing a swathe of mist.

'Mother of Mists!' Nandi sprang out of the water to welcome the old one, while Loiyan's eyes widened in astonishment. So this was the woman with the cauldron – she who had sustained her during the hard days and nights in the cavern.

'Daughters of my daughter!' Marumuruti's eyes were shining in her wrinkled face. 'So – it is done! I felt the waning of his power. Look – there go the plovers, and do you hear the bitterns rejoicing, and the night heron and my little egrets! Singing, all of them, crying out that Moloch is dead! The river will run sweet again and the air of our valleys will be free of malice and the webs of bitterness and envy. You have done well, daughters of my daughter. You have done very well.'

Marumuruti enfolded them in a warm embrace. Then she went and stood on a spit in the river shallows and turned to face the east where the Morning Star still shone faintly. She lifted her hands and she sang to the star a song so ancient that only she understood the words. And yet the tune of her song seemed somehow familiar to them and they found themselves singing too. At last the Morning Star faded and Marumuruti's arms fell to her sides. She gave a soft hooting call and a wood owl flew out of the trees to roost on her shoulder. After a brief conversation Kovankuni flew away into the high forest and Marumuruti said, 'The clans of Galuma will know that Moloch's reign is ended. Kinya and Kobel will have the tidings before sunset today and they will rejoice.'

As they stood there in the shallows the sun rose and Marumuruti gathered her cloak about her. 'It is time for you to return to your people. They are camped down there by the ford,' she pointed. 'And I know the eyes of at least two or three that are turned this way, waiting in hope!'

Loiyan turned to the old woman. 'Mother of Mists, I carry a whole gourd full of thanks; how can I pour it out if you send us away so soon?'

The old one patted her arm. 'I must go back to my cave, for there is always work for me. And yet … a great and long story is coming to an end now. The story of the Stone of Naiterogop that we have each woven a skein into, right to its very end. It must be told and it must be heard and remembered. At twilight of the third day from now, when the mist begins to creep along the valley, you must come to my cave. Bring your old people, the warriors and the children and the tale shall be told. Now hurry along and tell

Tajewo and Meromo that there is still honey beer in the cave of Marumuruti.' With a sweep of her cloak the old woman gathered the mists that lingered on the water behind her and disappeared.

Moipu ran ahead of them along a path beside the river until they came to a green valley ringed with trees. Smoke was rising from an early fire and a man stood near the trees alone, spear in hand, keeping watch. Tajewo gave a shout when Loiyan and Nandi came in sight and his cry brought the whole engang running to meet them. Lemeikoki was lifted from Tajewo's shoulders as Loiyan came running to meet them and she held him to her heart for a long moment, her eyes shining with joy. There, under the kranses of the river, where he had first heard the cold voice of Moloch and had feared for Loiyan and his people, Tajewo welcomed back the wife he loved and Meromo and Nandi held each other again.

There was so much to tell and so much to listen to that people only stopped talking to drink the sweet milk they craved. But before they walked home over the plains to build their homes again, they went at twilight to the Cave of Mists. Marumuruti told them the long tale of Naiterogop and the tear of the Morning Star. Each of them learned of their role in the great story and to each came the knowledge that they were not only the children of Naiterogop but that they were people who were favoured by a great one of the sky, the Morning Star himself.